SpringerWienNewYork

**CONSEQUENCE BOOK SERIES ON FRESH ARCHITECTURE
VOL. 7**

HERAUSGEGEBEN VON / EDITED BY
iCP - INSTITUTE FOR CULTURAL POLICY

SHAUN MURRAY
DISTURBING TERRITORIES

SpringerWienNewYork

iCP – Institute for Cultural Policy

Leitung / Direction:
Patrick Ehrhardt
Wolfgang Fiel

Öffentlichkeitsarbeit / Public relations:
Andrea Möller, Hamburg

www.i-c-p.org

Das Werk ist urheberrechtlich geschützt.
Die dadurch begründeten Rechte, insbesondere die der Übersetzung, des Nachdruckes, der Entnahme von Abbildungen, der Funksendung, der Wiedergabe auf photomechanischem oder ähnlichem Wege und der Speicherung in Datenverarbeitungsanlagen, bleiben, auch bei nur auszugsweiser Verwertung, vorbehalten.

This work is subject to copyright.
All rights are reserved, wheter the whole or part of the material is concerned, specifically those of translation, reprinting, re-use of illustrations, broadcasting, reproduction by photocoping machines or similar means, and storage in data banks.

© 2006 Springer-Verlag/Wien
Printed in Austria
SpringerWienNewYork is a part of
Springer Science+Business Media
springeronline.com

Die Wiedergabe von Gebrauchsnamen, Handelsnamen, Warenbezeichnungen usw. in diesem Buch berechtigt auch ohne besondere Kennzeichnung nicht zu der Annahme, dass solche Namen im Sinne der Warenzeichen- und Markenschutz-Gesetzgebung als frei zu betrachten wären und daher von jedermann benutzt werden dürften.

The use of registered names, trademarks, etc. in this publication does not imply, even in the absence of specific statement, that such names are exempt from the relevant protective laws and regulations and therefore free of general use.

Umschlagbilder Cover illustrations: © 2005 Shaun Murray
Layout: Andreas Berlinger; London / Lynwen Anthony; London
Druck Printing: Holzhausen Druck & Medien GmbH
1140 Wien, Österreich

Gedruckt auf säurefreiem, chlorfrei gebleichtem Papier - TCF
Printed on acid-free and chlorine-free bleached paper
SPIN: 11404286

Mit zahlreichen (großteils farbigen) Abbildungen
With numerous (mainly coloured) illustrations

Bibliografische Informationen Der Deutschen Bibliothek
Die Deutsche Bibliothek verzeichnet diese Publikation in der Deutschen Nationalbibliografie; detaillierte bibliografische Daten sind im Internet über <http://dnb.ddb.de> abrufbar.

ISBN-10 3-211-25245-2 SpringerWienNewYork
ISBN-13 978-3-211-25245-1 SpringerWienNewYork

Vorwort des Herausgebers
Consequence: Rendering the boundaries

`Is urban architecture in the process of becoming a technology just as outdated as extensive farming? Will architectonics become nothing more than a decadent form of dominating the earth, with consequences analogous to the unbridled exploitation of raw materials? Hasn't the decline in the number of cities also become the symbol of industrial decline and forced unemployment, the symbol of scientific materialism's failure? (...) The crisis of modernity's grand narratives, about which Lyotard speaks, betrays the presence of new technology, with the emphasis being placed, from now on, on the „means" and not on the „ends"´ (Virilio 1999).

In Anknüpfung an obiges Zitat von Paul Virilio gehen wir von der These aus, dass das Berufsbild der ArchitektIn einem grundsätzlichen poststrukturalistischen Wandel unterliegt. Mit der Immersion der digitalen Medien und elektronischen Apparate muss die Definition des architektonischen Raums einer grundsätzlichen und zeitgemäßen Revision unterzogen werden. Während das psychische Modell des modernistischen Raumparadigmas mit der Echzeiterfahrung im physischen Realraum noch kongruent war und durch die Regeln der klassischen Perspektive hinreichend beschrieben werden konnte, führt die rhizomatische Organisation der Datennetzwerke an den Schnittstellen global verteilter Userterminals zum Verlust der Wahrnehmung räumlicher Tiefe zugunsten einer kinematografischen Zeittiefe. Die Ästhetik stabiler Bilder wird durch die Ästhetik des beschleunigten Verschwindens labiler Bilder ersetzt. Räumliche Exploration erfolgt nunmehr weltumspannend an jedem beliebigen Ort, während Simultanität in elastischen Zeitintervallen erfolgt und durch die „Trägheit des Auges" bestimmt wird.

Das heisst aber auch, dass wir einen Paradigmenwechsel von der Repräsentation zur Interpretation vollziehen, der eng mit der Frage nach der Konstituierung brauchbarer Schnittstellen verbunden ist. Die von Virilio angesprochene Verlagerung von der Zielfunktion (ends) zur Wahl der Mittel (means) im Rahmen einer prozesshaften Kultur des Ereignisses entspricht gleichzeitig einer Verschiebung von der Metaebene eines dialektischen Theoriebegriffs zur mikropolitischen Praxis improvisatorischen Handelns.

Mit der Auswahl der im Rahmen der Ausstellungsreihe „consequence" präsentierten ArchitektInnen soll die gängige Praxis gegenwärtiger Architekturproduktion hinterfragt werden. Sie verkörpern auf exemplarische Weise die vielfältigen Ausdrucksformen im Zuge der skizzierten Neudefinition des Berufsbilds. Die jeweiligen Tätigkeitsfelder sind durch die systematische Entwicklung partikularer Forschungsschwerpunkte gekennzeichnet, einer Art mikropolitischer und methodischer Praxis an den Rändern der eigenen Profession sowie im transdisziplinären Crossover unterschiedlicher Disziplinen. Die Arbeitsweisen haben einen Hang zum Technologischen, sind narrativ, performativ, spekulativästhetisch und verfügen über ein Problembewusstsein, das auf einer konzeptuellen Ebene verankert ist oder am spezifischen Kontext festgemacht werden kann. Mit der Auswahl soll auf eine Generation aufmerksam gemacht werden, die mit ihren Arbeiten neue diskursive Räume erschließt.

Wolfgang Fiel, Hamburg, Juni 2005

Virilio, P 1999, `The overexposed city´, in Druckrey, T. & Ars Electronica (eds.), *Facing The Future*, MIT Press, Cambridge, pp. 276-283.

Editorial Notice
Consequence: Rendering the boundaries

`Is urban architecture in the process of becoming a technology just as outdated as extensive farming? Will architectonics become nothing more than a decadent form of dominating the earth, with consequences analogous to the unbridled exploitation of raw materials? Hasn't the decline in the number of cities also become the symbol of industrial decline and forced unemployment, the symbol of scientific materialism's failure? (...) The crisis of modernity's grand narratives, about which Lyotard speaks, betrays the presence of new technology, with the emphasis being placed, from now on, on the „means" and not on the „ends"´ (Virilio 1999).

Following up to the statement from Paul Virilio, the claim is set out, that the profession of the architect currently undergoes a significant post-structuralist change. With the immersion of digital media and electronic apparatus the definition of physical space and its perception has to be fundamentally revised. Whilst the psychological imprint of the modernistic dimension of space was specified by significant „time distances" in relation to physical obstacles, represented by the rules of perspective, the rhizomatic nature of electronic networks - accessable via the interfaces of globally distributed userterminals – has subsequently led to the loss of spatial depth in exchange for the cinematic depth of time. The believe in the enduring objectives of dualistic determinism has been succeeded by an aesthetic of the accelerated disappearance of transient images. The exhaustion of temporal distance creates a telescoping of any localization, at any position and any time, for it simultaneity is measured in elastic time-intervals equivalent to the retinal persistance - the after image.

Likewise we face a paradigmatic change from the era of representation to one of interpretation which is closely bound to the need of creating operable interfaces. In the light of the turn from the „ends" to the „means" as aforementioned, a process-oriented culture of events would cause an improvisational turn from the meta-level of the dialectic theory-notion toward a micropolitical practice.

With the choice of architects within the scope of „consequence", well established modernistic modes of architectural representation are challenged. All of these architects embody a wide range of formal expression, as a result of their unique endeavour in research and architectonic practice alike. Their particular fields of activity are characterized by a tentative policy in exploring and augmenting the boundaries of the profession as well as to foster a prolific interchange with other disciplines. The modes of operation are technological, often do follow narratives, are performative, speculative in their account for novel aesthetics and demonstrate a sensible awareness for current local phenomena and global developments, which can be tied to a specific context or are expressed on a conceptual level. With the choice for fresh accounts from a new generation of experimental architects, we aim to launch new territories of discourse.

Wolfgang Fiel, Hamburg, June 2005

Virilio, P. 1999, `The overexposed city´, in Druckrey, T. & Ars Electronica (eds.), *Facing The Future*, MIT Press, Cambridge, pp. 276-283.

Über / About iCP

Das `Institute for Cultural Policy´, wurde 2004 als unabhängige und interdisziplinäre Forschungseinrichtung in Hamburg/Deutschland gegründet. Das iCP bietet die Infrastruktur und ist diskursive Plattform für die Förderung und Weiterentwicklung des Austausches zwischen Architektur, Kunst, Wissenschaft und Industrie.

The `Institute for Cultural Policy´, was founded in 2004 as an independent and cross-disciplinary research institution in Hamburg/Germany. The iCP provides the infrastructure and is a platform for discourse fostering a prolific exchange between architecture, art, science and industry.

Kooperationen / Cooperations

Die Ausstellung mit dem gleichlautenden Titel vom 08.06. - 09.07.2006 im iCP, Hamburg ist eine Veranstaltung im Rahmen des Hamburger Architektur Sommer 2006. The exhibition with the same title from 08.06. - 09.07.2006 at the iCP, Hamburg is an event within the framework of the Hamburger Architektur Sommer 2006.

Hamburger Architektur Sommer 2006

Danksagung / Acknowledgements

Die Herausgeber bedanken sich bei allen, die am Zustandekommen des Projekts beteiligt waren, im Speziellen Lynwen Anthony, Alexandra Berlinger, Andreas Berlinger, Amelie Graalfs, Kathrin Harder, David Marold (SpringerWienNewYork) sowie Shaun Murray für die ausgezeichnete Zusammenarbeit.

Störung als Dynamo

Unter dem Einsatz sog. Neuer Technologien haben sich die architektonische Forschung und Praxis radikal verändert. Die dabei entstandene virtuelle Diaspora schöpft aus dem Möglichkeitsraum digitaler Repräsentationsformen und manifestiert sich als Ästhetik mit globalem Wiedererkennungswert. Wird für den Formgebungsprozess das beinahe unbegrenzte Ausmaß systemimmanenter Freiheit ausgelotet, sind die einzelnen Schritte selten Gegenstand einer bewertenden Analyse mit allfälligen Korrekturen. Sich mit dieser passiven Reflektions-Ästhetik zu bescheiden macht formale Kriterien von Zufälligkeiten abhängig, die sich in letzter Konsequenz nur noch mit der schieren Existenz und Anwendung technischer Möglichkeiten rechtfertigen lassen. Auf der Suche nach alternativen Paradigmen drängen sich Fragen nach dem Wiederentdecken von determinierten, absichtsvollen oder gar unvermeidlichen formalen Attributen auf, die den Entwurfsprozess und den Lebenszyklus gebauter Architektur gleichermaßen informieren. In vielen Fällen handelt es sich um ein Zusammenspiel mehrerer Faktoren, die derartige Attribute an ihren Schnittstellen erkennen lassen. In diesem Sinn konstituieren bauliche Struktur, jeweiliger Kontext (ökologische Rahmenbedingungen) und potentielle Nutzer ein dynamisches System, dessen bestimmende Eigenschaften relationaler Natur sind. Der architektonische Evolutionsbegriff wird vom funktionalen Verständnis für die gegebene Organisationsform bestimmt. Interpretiert als System mit wechselseitigen symbiotischen Abhängigkeitsverhältnissen zwischen den einzelnen Systemkomponenten, erhebt sich unweigerlich die Frage, inwieweit Architektur hinkünftig in der Lage sein wird, reflexives Verhalten an den Tag zu legen und damit als lebendiger Organismus definiert werden kann. Um dem naheliegenden Schluss zu entgehen, architektonische Entwicklung mit biologischer Evolution gleichzusetzen, mag es hilfreich sein, einen alternativen Zugang in die Diskussion einzubringen.

In seinem Buch `Was ist Leben?´ ist Schrödinger (1944) der Frage nachgegangen, welches Prinzip einen lebenden Organismus überlebensfähig macht, seine Entropie dabei relativ konstant bleibt und mit dem Zweiten Hauptsatz der Thermodynamik vereinbar ist? Er hat dazu den Begriff der `negativen Entropie´ eingeführt, die jeder lebende Organismus kontinuierlich seiner Umgebung entzieht. Demzufolge war für ihn der

Schlüssel zum Leben: `Ordnung durch Ordnung´. In Ergänzung zu Schrödingers Konzept hat von Foerster (1960) den zweiten Schlüssel zum Leben wie folgt formuliert: `Ordnung durch Störung´.

Der Ansatz von Shaun Murray könnte in diesem Sinn verstanden werden, da das Ökosystem seiner Projekte nicht nur deren strukturelle Veränderung bedingt, sondern darüber hinaus auch jene Störungen spezifiziert, die derartige Veränderungen auslösen. Er charakterisiert diesen Ansatz als Architektur "gekoppelter Aktionen", für die ihre Umgebung gewissermaßen einen genetischen Fingerabdruck kreiert. Auf diese Weise werden die Entstehungsbedingungen des architekonischen Objekts im Rahmen seines Bildungsvorgangs determiniert und können als Korrektiv einer kontinuierlichen Anpassung verstanden werden. Daraus zu folgern, dass architektonische Evolution durch Kriterien der Selektion und Anpassung gleichermaßen bestimmt wird, liefert entscheidende Hinweise für die Bewertung des „ökologischen Settings". Die Randbedingungen informieren einerseits den formalen Prozess und tragen andererseits dem Wunsch nach Dynamik und Veränderung gebauter Architektur durch permanente Interaktion mit dem jeweiligen Kontext Rechnung. Ob nun dieser Veränderungsprozess notwendigerweise als unmittelbar biologisches „Werden" oder als Mimesis im Sinne einer eigenständigen „Schöpfung" gilt, bleibt offen. Die Frage inwieweit materialistische Ökologien in Kombination mit dem biologischen Paradigma dem permanenten Veränderungsdruck gerecht werden können, stellt vielleicht eine der Herausforderungen für kommende Architektur dar.

Wolfgang Fiel, Wien, Mai 2006.

Foerster, Hv 1960, `Über selbst-organisierende Systeme und ihre Umwelten´, *Sicht und Einsicht*, Carl-Auer-Systeme Verlag, Heidelberg, pp.115-130.
Schrödinger, E 1944, `Ordnung, Unordnung und Entropie´, *Was ist Leben?*, Piper, München, pp.120-132.

Disturbance as dynamo

Through the application of so-called New Technologies, architectural research and practice has undergone radical changes. The resulting virtual diaspora scoops from the wide realm of possible digital representation and becomes manifest as aesthetics of global trade. Given, that for the process of form generation the almost limitless scale of freedom immanent to the system is fully endorsed, each single step is seldomly subject to an analytic evaluation and subsequent modification. Giving in to this reflective and passive notion of aesthetics does necessarily lead to formal randomness, for it the final results may often be justified by the sheer existence and application of a technical possibility only. This raises questions about alternative paradigms that seek to rediscover the precisely determined, purposeful, or inevitable attributes of form, that would inform the design process and the life cycle of built architecture likewise. In many cases this involves an interplay of several factors, that come to the fore at their interfaces. In this particular case the built structure, its given context (ecological parameters) and its potential users constitute a dynamic system whose decisive properties are of relational nature. The architectural notion of evolution is governed by a functional apprehension of the given adhocracy. Interpreted as system with mutual symbiotic interdependence between its distict constituting components, the question has to be raised, in how far architecture will be in a position for reflexive behaviour and could therefore be classified as living organism. In order to avoid the obvious deduction in identifying architectural growth with the biological concept of evolution, it might be instructive to consider an alternative approach for further discussion.

In his book entitled `What is life´, Schrödinger (1944) has speculated about the basic principle at work, that keeps the entropy of a living organism relatively constant and would comply to the second law of thermodynamics. He coined the term `negative entropy´, that each living organism would have to detract from the environment continually. Subsequently for him the key to life was: `Order by Order´.Complemental to Schrödingers concept Foerster (1960) proposed what he called `second key to life: Order by disturbance´. This might bo the starting point to gain a more comprehensive understanding of Shaun Murray's conceptual framework. Not only determines the ecosystem of his projects their structural modifications, it also specifies which disturbances from the environment trigger them. He characterises this concept as an architecture of „coupled actions" with the environment creating a genetic fingerprint. The conditions for the creation of architectural objects are determined through the very process and furthermore act as corrective in the course of continual adaptation. Reasoning that architectural evolution is governed by criteria of selection and adaptation likewise, does provide decisive clues to essess the given ecological setting. The restraints inform the formal process on the one hand and wing hope to the idea of having an architecture that once built remains dynamic because of its interaction with the given environmental context. Whether this process of permanent modification alludes to an immediate „becoming" or to mimesis in terms of autonomous creation is left open. The question how far materialistic ecologies combined with the biological paradigm are able to meet the requirements of permanent modification may be the challenge for future architecture.

Wolfgang Fiel, Vienna, May 2006.

Foerster, Hv 1960, `Über selbst-organisierende Systeme und ihre Umwelten´, *Sicht und Einsicht*, Carl-Auer-Systeme Verlag, Heidelberg, pp.115-130.
Schrödinger, E 1944, `Ordnung, Unordnung und Entropie´, *Was ist Leben?*, Piper, München, pp.120-132.

How do you denote notation to the rhythms of the outside world, some of self-absorbing intuitive and poetic architecture acting out a battle with the limits…

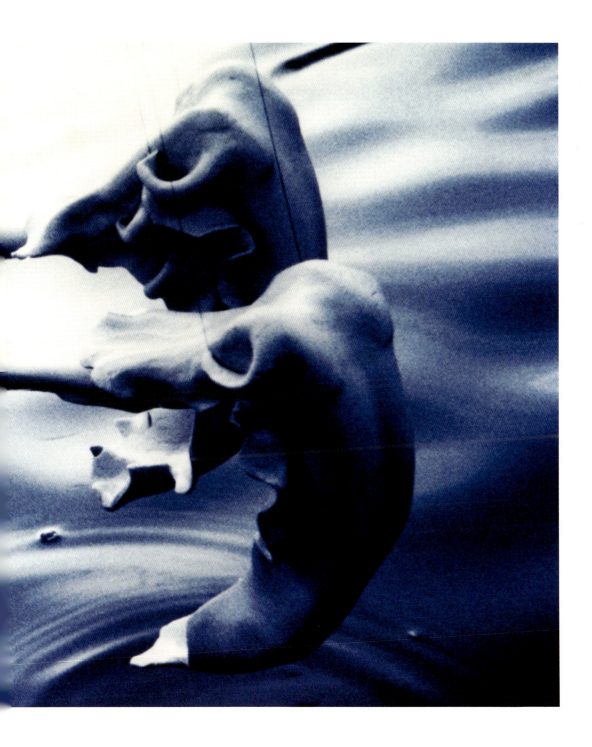

Contents

8	Introduction – Shaun Murray
20	Forword – Neil Spiller The Digitised Ecological Architecture of Shaun Murray
28	Camargue Ecology
70	On Becoming Ecology
90	Archulus Ecology
107	Afterword – **Roy Ascott** Gardens of Hypotheses and Geomediated Meaning
116	Glossary
120	Conclusion
122	Acknowledgements

Introduction

"The myth of power is of course, a very powerful myth; and probably most people in this world more or less believe in it... But it is still epistemological lunacy and leads inevitably to all sorts of disaster... To want control is the pathology! Not that a person can get control, because of course you never do... Man is only a part of larger systems, and the part can never control the whole". (Gregory Bateson 1972)

With the impact of virtual technologies the study and practice of architecture has rapidly changed. Through new techniques in drawing, communication and language allow even the most normative practice to enjoy complete freedom. This arbitrariness and lack of restraint that characterises this new era of formal freedom raises questions about other paradigms that seek to rediscover the precisely determined, purposeful, or inevitable attributes of form. A guide would be to not clamber for control over these techniques and technologies but allow the architecture to become apart of larger systems through disturbing territories.

The ecology of the projects not only specifies its structural changes it also specifies which disturbances from the environment trigger them. According to Humberto Maturana and Francisco Varela, you can never direct a living system; you can only disturb it.

One is the notion of a building existing in the form intended as a result of complex inter-relationship with it, or through it, or on it, where the building itself exists in the relationships between things, not the thing themselves.

The other is the reflexive space of the building itself through cause and action being triggered by the occupant or disturbances in the environment.

Territories

Territories imply occupation and interaction. Territories offer entry to notational space, structuring drawing into a relationship with environment. Territories are an instrument for navigation and organisation with user – reader – space. As architecture seeks to rediscover form, territories seek to occupy and interact from within. Territories in the dictionary are defined areas, including land and waters, usually considered to be a possession of an animal, person, organization, or institution from the word terra, meaning land.

In biology, an organism which defends an area against intrusion (usually from members of its own species) is said to be territorial. In psychology, environmentalists study territorial behaviour to understand which territory an organism defends and why. Territorial behaviour is defined as the actions or reactions of a person or animal in response to external threats towards the space that is defended by that person or animal. Territories are not defined by a fence or line but are dynamic and transformative forever interacting with the boundaries between the natural and artificial. The fact that when drawing can fully exchange information with natural phenomena, architecture's capabilities for knowledge and communication would be far deeper and more extended than presently understood. It also would disturb the boundary lines of our individuality – our very sense of separateness with the built environment.

Overview

With the range of the various definitions of the term territories, and through the title of this book I intend to define the contents. The projects and essays found within five years combine to propose a different way of thinking about the relationships between drawing and environment, and the states between. A direct way of approaching this subject matter is to bring the notions of territories and spatiality together in a discussion about purpose and rigour in the digital and pre biophysical age.

Suspending Process

The beginnings of this process of thinking started in 1999 with my diploma project Camargue Condensations, presented as design portfolio and as a theoretical dissertation at the Bartlett School of Architecture, University College London, England. Consequently, I went on to complete a Masters project Archulus Flood Structure at the Bartlett School of Architecture. Then I came across Ilya Prigogine and Isabelle Stengers' book Order out of Chaos: Man's new dialogue with nature from 1984. Prigogine suggests a theory in relation to the study of the natural phenomena exhibited around us – in our terrestrial environment upon this earth, and in the local cosmic environment within which the terrestrial is embedded. Prigogine and Stengers invoke the roman poet Lucretius, with his urge to look for the hidden behind the obvious. "Sometimes", wrote Lucretius, "at uncertain times and places, the eternal, universal fall of the atoms is disturbed by a very slight deviation – the clinamen. The resulting vortex gives rise to the world, to all natural things.
(Ilya Prigogine 1984)

After spending some years studying the ideas proposed in Order out of Chaos: Man's new dialogue with nature, I arrived in 2003 with a host of projects that resulted in a series of articles Breeding – Feeding – Leeching, Assimilating Environments, A priori Nature: Constructing Architectures, Reflexive Practice in Architectural Ecologies and Coupling Fields: towards an Ecological Architecture of Linkages.

The approach is based on that part of communications theory which Bertrand Russell (Whitehead and Russell 1910) has called the Theory of Logical Types. The central thesis of this theory is that there is a discontinuity between a class and its members. The class cannot be a member of itself nor can one of the members be the class, since the term used for the class is of a different level of abstraction – a different Logical Type – from terms used for members. Although in formal logic there is an attempt to maintain the discontinuity between a class and its members, I argue that in architecture of real communications this discontinuity is continually breached. And that a priori we must expect pathology to occur in the process of a project when certain formal patterns of the breaching occur in the communication between drawing and environment. I argue that this process at its extreme will have approaches whose characteristics would lead the process to be classified as meaningless.

Apriori model 01

Apriori model 02

Apriori model 03

Apriori model 04

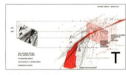
Apriori model 05

Apriori model 06

B Construct

K Construct

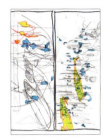
Apriori model 10

Apriori model 09

Apriori model 08

Apriori model 07

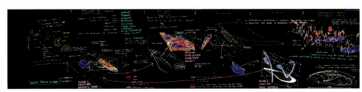
Apriori model 11

Illustrations of how practice methodologies handle communication involving multiple Logical Types can be derived from the following fields:

1. The use of various research projects from my own practice which comprise of Apriori model 01 – 11, B Construct and K Construct (see previous page).
All these models explore how one can suspend 'process' to reveal the development of various forms suspended along the continuum of a project. The method of exploration involves the use of notations which are characterised by levels of Logical Types or communicational modes.

2. Other practices, through working at Will Alsop practice and John Coward Architects. This seems to be a method of exploring the tacit knowledge through the process of a project. The method of exploration involves the use of messages which are characterised by a condensation of Logical Types or communicational modes. Through process the development of form is suspended along the continuum of the project. The most identifiable outcome is the physical construct, but on some projects the form could be suspended in conversation or during a meeting.

3. In the series of workshops completed with Arch-OS in the University of Plymouth, the students operated at multiple levels of learning and the Logical Typing of signals. These are two inseparable sets of phenomena – inseparable because the ability to handle the multiple types of signals is itself a learned skill and therefore a function of the multiple level of learning. Arch-OS is an operating system for buildings developed to manifest the social, technological and environmental use of a building to its users. It is to provide artists, engineers, and scientists with a facility for transdisciplinary research and production. Arch-OS was integrated into the fabric of the University of Plymouth's Portland Square Building, which houses the headquarters of the Institute for Digital Art and Technology (i-DAT). The process of the workshops bifurcated into multiple tracks, for example, notational through drawing, tacit knowledge through communication and reflexive through installations.

4. Research groups at the Bartlett School of Architecture, University College London, England and Brighton University, England. Using process in a design project to reveal the relata between drawing and environment. Exploring how process can cause failure of the development of form suspended along the continuum of a project.

5. Response to Theory and Practice. To critique the field in relation to process, to be able to move forward by stating that there is another thing that is important, which is the critique on drawing which is imperative for an alternative agenda. Can we map this territory for a theory of suspending process?

Current practice methodologies in architecture have become a series of systems of operations. In the architectural model the plan has become obsolete as a vehicle to understand the axis of information production towards the construction of a building and the axis of post building systems which are incorporated after building completion.

My argument is for a process that works around this current model as a way of connecting the user – reader – space in a more holistic sense. The model I am using is an Ecotype Map, which becomes a way of thinking about the relationships between drawing and environment and the states between. It is through drawing notational systems I want to examine the state of transfer from one medium, as drawing, to another, as environment, as in a material transfer or fortuitous transfer. This model may be understood as the syncretism of user – reader – space through communication between states, field and notational systems. To develop what will essentially become the framework of steps to architecture on becoming ecology. By this approach, to grasp the essential framework of user – reader – space through the developments in drawing notation directly towards steps to architecture on becoming ecology. But the definition of architecture on becoming ecology which the projects and essays combine to propose is much wider and more formal than is conventional. The projects must speak for themselves, but here at the beginning let me state my belief that such matters as, dialogue with nature, transformation, concepts of relationships between the user – reader – space can only be understood as disturbing these territories as I propose. And it is essentially through the drawing that I currently claim for 'architecture ecology'. It is hoped the practice work will develop to the next step and embody the environment directly, so we can seek to rediscover the precisely determined, purposeful, or inevitable attributes of form.

Ecotype Map

"The map is not the territory." Alford Korzybski

As Michael Polyani has written, "all theory is a kind of map." Thus we are left in the situation of mapping the map. We are at least setting up conditions for a highly complimentary of interactivist relationship between map and territory when dealing with the conceptual realm. An ecotype map is characterised by the surroundings it inhabits. It can be divided into Logical Types, as described above, as levels in the drawing rather like a palimpsest. Different levels develop distinct physiological characteristics in response to a specific environment which persist even if a level is moved to a different environment.

In a performance the communication from composer (user), to performer (reader) or environment (space) is not at all straightforward. That architecture is reaching from the mental to the physical world must pass through a process of visualisation, alienating itself from pure architecture. Notation has made the composition of architecture an activity like the composition of fiction: the activity of communication. So deep is the connection between architecture and communication in our culture that for much of the time we ignore it and behave as if notation were really a transparent window. Just as in reading a drawing we may ignore the intermediacy of notation and imagine that thoughts are reaching us directly from the architect's mind. The most important criterion of algorithms, whether literally or architectural, is precisely that it should not draw attention to itself, not disturb the illusion of neutrality and faithfulness.

Similar to Bateson, let me shift from a musical to a wider biological analogy in order to examine further this magical realm of communication. All organisms are partially determined by genetics, i.e., by complex constellations of messages carried principally in the chromosomes. We are products of a communication process, modified and qualified in various ways by environmental impact. A change in the message may be one which modifies or modulates the whole system of genetic messages, so that every message in the system takes on a different look while retaining its former relationship to all neighbouring messages.

These interactions of the logical types of the drawing and environment together form a spatial unit, which is termed an ecotype. This system is defined as a unit of interaction with the physical environment so that a flow of energy leads to a clearly defined notational, instructional and aesthetical neologism.

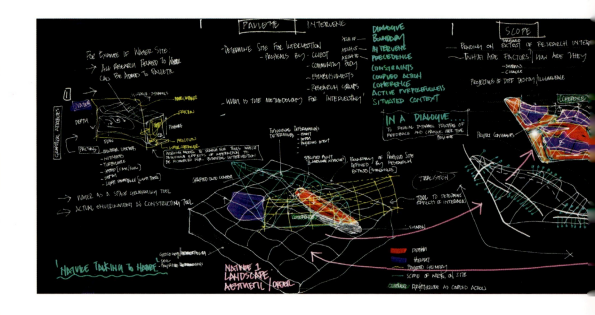

Ecotype Map

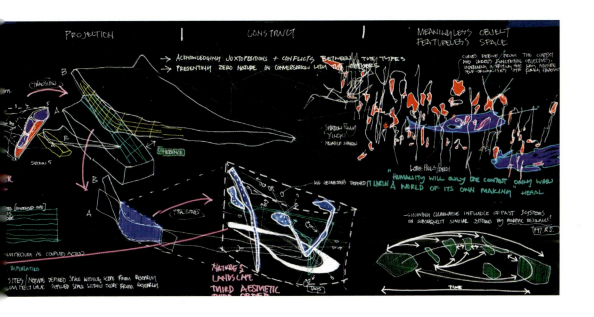

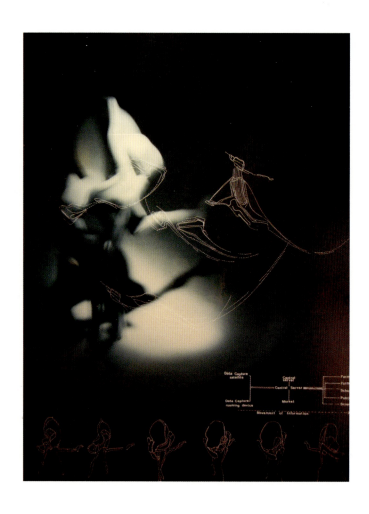

Information Polyp showing distributed network

The Digitised Ecological Architecture of Shaun Murray – Neil Spiller

Shaun is one of the very few architects that I have considerable respect for. He is tenacious, dogged and highly ambitiously self motivated. He combines these traits with a dry Northern wit, which can become animated after a few pints. He like many Northerners cannot bear injustice or Southern esoteric posturing. He does the 'bizz' and he expects everyone else to. Often his lean form, honed by mile upon mile of cycled navigation through London's byways and back ways, seems taut with creativity attempting to force itself out of him and him attempting to keep it in until it is fully gestated.

Shaun was a student of my and Phil Watson's Diploma unit 19 at the Bartlett in the late nineteen nineties. A unit that sought to fully explore the impact of advanced technology on architectural design, and it still does. I remember his student peer group being on the whole pretty talented and this imperative to perform fired the young Liverpool based undergraduate and formed him into a speculative and enquiring Bartlett student. Shaun handled the culture shock of the Bartlett swiftly and effectively. Perhaps the first real indication of the work to come was his quick project "Information Polyp" that was linked via geo satellite to remote computers, driven by the vicissitudes of the wind would create a kind of alternative geography of points and observations. A kind of weird Duchampian "Stoppage" for the digital age. A mixed reality yardstick for the benchmarking of the Information Superhighway.

Turbulence, Skirts and Tusks

This fecund starting point was soon to develop into a full-blown proposition for a series of architectural pieces, each individually tailored for their immediate context yet all spatially embroidered, thus creating a suite of highly sensile, ascalarly nested, neurotic, geographically diverse, delicate networked structures. This extraordinary project entitled "Carmargue Condensations" became one of the iconic works produced by the Bartlett at this time. The Carmargue in Southern France with its horses, the Mistral wind and the Rhone-Soane rivers, the saltpans and the rugged inhabitants is a romantic site to choose. Shaun's personally set task was to explore this physical geography of romanticism and combine it with the global information technology that at the time was beginning to network us together: animal and vegetable and crystal. So the project is like some great prosthesis that allows the users/inhabitants to feel the ecological ripples of their immediate and also remote environs, like wired pond skaters.

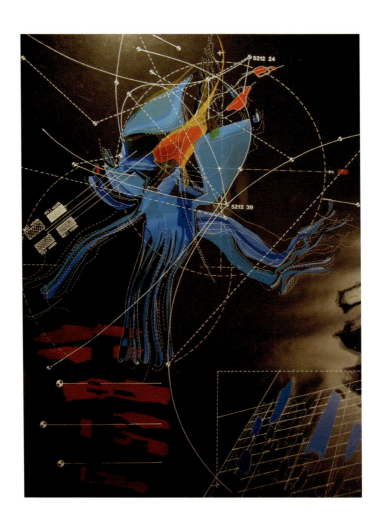

Information Polyp trajectories with skin detail

The project deals with various phenomenological architectural conditions: mediation of the ground line, for example, is addressed with dune like enclosures. The underworld of prehistoric cave art is penetrated by light cages, which illuminate yet, which also protect the art from the destabilising glare of artificial light. A gaping calanque which can flash flood has two tusk-like small buildings with a light skirt inserted and strung above it. The floodwaters act like enlivening lifeblood to. When soaked it writhes like a fish with its head in a vice. Also a series or artful kites sup at the spiralling vortex of the Mistral. So the local contextural integration of the pieces is established in this elemental way. On top of this local contextuality is the spatial embroidery that flips scales, links this to that and make each small architectural piece a microcosm of the great macrocosmic whole. This of course is what we now experience in our day to day life: the conic sections of vision are no longer conic, we can see far, wide, deep and all engrossingly. The whole of the work is again networked into what one might call a master complex. Where both machinic and natural ecologies can be recorded, gleaned and seen in relation to human use patterns and surprises.

Harpoonic Landscapes

In the later Archulus project Shaun picks another delicate ecology, teetering on the edge of oblivion. The sudden critical act is again used as a trigger for action. Like the sodden tusks that are suddenly enlivened into movement the Archulus project is enlivened by physical collapse. In this certain area of East Anglia in England a small spit of land that separates the sea from the local river is being eroded from both sides simultaneously. At a certain point in the not so distant future the spit will collapse and its primitive flood defence will be breached. This moment Shaun picks for the sudden genesis of a new landscape that becomes into being in the time it takes for a series of harpoons to fire their elegant spikes into the sea. These harpoons then anchor the new landscape surface. The surface then, in effect, terraforms itself and encourages a rich mix of new colonising flora and fauna. Out of catastrophe a rebirth takes place, not the same as before but different, and the consequent flooding of the old spit's hinterland is averted.

These two projects are a harbinger for a meaningful ecological (both machinic and natural) audit of specific sites and the development of a series of tactics and protocols that can deliver to architects a full under provide architects with these now very necessary tools for them to create architectures that are fully in tune with the wide gamut of artificial and natural ecological conditions. For those of us interested in the architecture for the new cyberised, biomachined inhabitants of the twenty-first century Shaun's research and propositions are a beacon in a still dark landscape of the future.

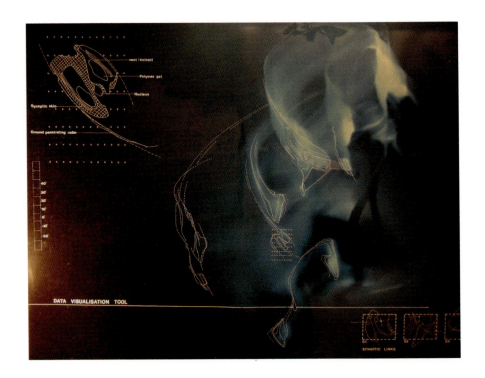

Information Polyp as data visualisation tool

Not only has Shaun developed this interesting and original approach to architecture and ecology but he has also developed various methods of representing architecture. Like any architect who deals explicitly with the ravages of time, and the choreography of sudden and not so sudden shifts in geography and geometry have to be charted. Shaun has needed to generate a draughting style that facilitates and explains his ideas. His drawings are multi-layered, highly wrought, not for him the simple sharkskin aesthetic of computer renderings with their reductivist pseudo materiality. He is a master of the plain old-fashioned airbrush, the dotted line that delineates trajectory, twist and pause. His perspectives are low slung and expose the ground plain, very much a Dali or Yves Tanguy would. This interest in matters surrealist has also indicated itself in Shaun's preoccupation with Roberto Matta's strange hyper geometry paintings of the 1940's and these can be seen to follow similar aspirations as Shaun's – that of the different realities and their wormholes draw on the same piece of terrain. Bifurcating systems coalescing, bonding exchanging and splitting as all things do!

This monograph I hope will be received well and I hope Shaun's influence on the next generation of architects will grow and through it his important work will not be lost and overlooked. We would be silly indeed if such a thing happened. Enjoy this book and marvel at a talent still being forged and watch Shaun's evolution into a force to be reckoned with on the international stage.

I wish him luck with a sense of admiration.

Neil Spiller is Professor of Architecture and Digital Theory, Bartlett School of Architecture.

Camargue Ecology

Rhône Valley, Southeast France

The Rhone Valley and adjacent river is for me the subject of certain chronic mental wanderings, clinical enough in nature to produce these drawings, models and explanatory text you are now reading. One of them concerns a vacillating object floating in the Gorge du Fier and becomes animated during annual flood conditions one week in September.

There are four locations stretched down the Rhône, each of the locations enable the user to read the environment through the architectures which are in accordance to the four elemental forces of Water, Earth, Fire and Wind.

This project reverberates around a series of 'split' sites linked to each other within a complex web of feedback loops and retrosensing devices. It centres on the harnessing of natural phenomena, complex ecological networks within the unique environmental conditions of the Rhone valley in southern France. By making use of modern technologies, including caged light and magnetorheorological compounds, these naturally fluid systems will be amplified and distorted to form self-regulating, interactive configurations, with endless possibilities for adaptation and transformation. As well as collecting and collating ecological information for research uses, this network provides the means for the user as reader, to be 'plugged into' nature. At various critical locations the user becomes yet another component of the network, influencing the environment; and simultaneously being acted on by diverse factors. These architectures are distributed across sensitive geomorphologically and ecologically special locations, such as gorges that flash flood, salt pans or the point of the France's thinnest Earth's crust, all of which are along the Rhone corridor that terminates at the Camargue and is prone to the ravages of the mistral wind. Within these frameworks intricate mechanisms will form hyperaesthetic connections, augmented, distorted sensations and an immersive intensity orator for a personal dialogue with the modern tourist. The synthesis between the locations will have an extensive impact on this sensitive landscape beyond their immediate location, disturbing the threshold between the natural and the artificial.

The key points to be discussed in the following project are firstly to introduce each node through materiality and the relationship with its natural trigger in each of the five locations. Following that I will discuss the relationship between user – reader – space in the drawing environment and describe what territories are disturbed by altering the states between the natural and the artificial. This will be explained through each node individually and then collectively how one node will effect the other tectonically and spatially.

Water
Gorges du Fier

Les Gorges du Fier, at 300 metres long and 60 metres deep, is classified among the largest curiosities of the Alps. Inside these throats one can admire a giant pot of water. To the exit is the impressive aspect of la mer des rochers, a labyrinth eroded by the river le Fier. Along the vertical faces is a scale showing the heights reached by the river in flood, including September 1960, when it rose 27m above its normal level.

The gallery allows the user to scrutinise without any danger the depth of the abyss, where the river Le Fier scours and groans. Beneath your feet is the smart floor which aims to identify and track you around the labyrinth of walkways, measuring other biometric features, such as weight, gait distance, and gait period to assist identification. This information is used to establish the intensity of the experience and the altered state of effects in the vacillating object. There are different sensors connecting different actions of visitors to fluidity. Light, touch and pulling sensors respectively creating the vector, the inflection and the frame in real time projection, real time sound manipulation and the interference of the light sp(l)ine with its information projectiles. Between animated elements a projected space allows the user to experience a disturbance in the territories.

The cradles swing out from the gallery and present the user to the point of immersion into the watery throats of the gorge and the vacillating object. They are now an active participant in disturbing the field whilst swaying inside the two cradles. Swinging out over the gorge below the cradles connect into the vacillating object. Once the user is inside the vacillating object the pressure-sensitive floor will trigger a silicon glow around the cradle to show it has become activated. The colour of the light is tuned pending on the particular absorption and emission of activities in the fire node. Within the cradle the user listens for visual signals from the other nodes through the phonoscope, which acts as an instrument for the translation of sound vibrations into visible images.

The vacillating object operates between the user and the environment. This notion creates a second order field where the user communicates not directly with the environment but through a reader of the environment as a user. The vacillating objects are fixed within the central axis of the gorge, allowing the turbulent water to pass through it, or on it, where the vacillating object itself exists in the relationship between things. Along the length of the sp(l)ine is a series of information projectiles. The displays retain a ring of water spouts which can be inflated and deflated through a series of release gates which can be opened to spurt out water when the pressure is too great. This assembly in each array will be fitted

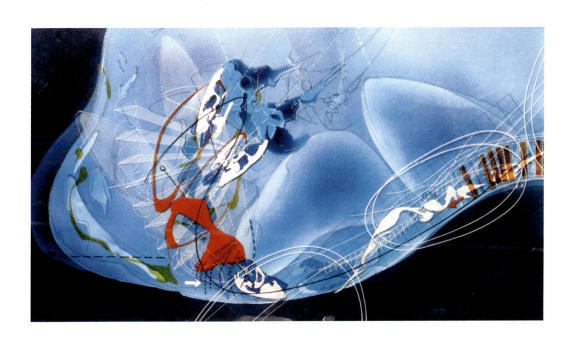

Aerial view of Gorges Du Fier

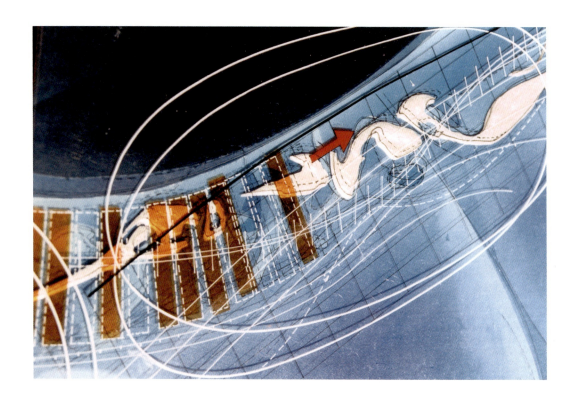

Gallery detail

Cradle detail

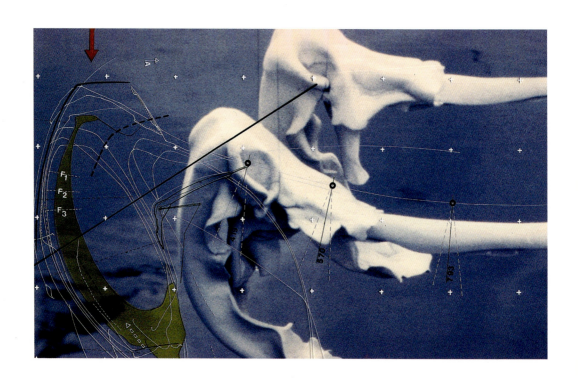

Vacillating Object with section detail

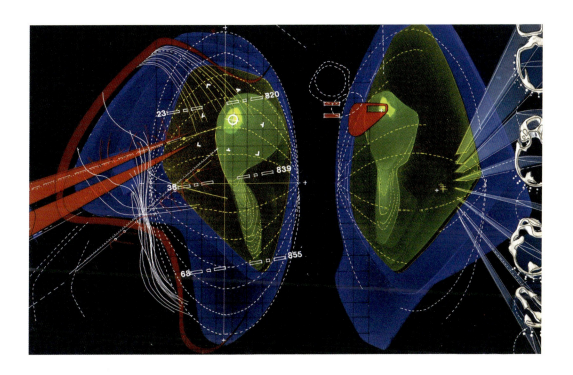

Tripper view inside the Vacillating Object

with a micro processor. Output from the system will be used to sustain the vacillating objects mobility. The tripper can slide down on a calibrated foot-track from the cradle into the guts of the vacillating object which can be calibrated to enable each individual user to gaze into the throat through the sp(l)ine. Now the user counter balances the physical weight of the vacillating object to becomes apart of it. Once located inside, the user is presented with three mathematically related images through different filters via a digital interface, described as F1, F2 and F3. Respectively each image has been adjusted to present other sites in real time, act as an instrument for translating sound vibrations into visible images and a pressure-sensitive backrest which controls the light source along the length of the sp(l)ine. All three filters adjust the vasodilator which acts like a muscle as you gaze through it.

Slung out behind the vacillating object is the generated texture field, which comprises of a fine meshed net. The net continually flows with the surface topology of the water. The notion of delay is introduced where the flow of the net could be controlled by some external agent. Contained within the wires of the net are magnetorheological fluids which can be switched to a highly viscous or semisolid gel-like state in a matter of a few thousandths of a second by applying a strong magnetic current. This smart net can be made intelligent by coupling it to sensor devices which, for example, detect sudden fluctuations such as those caused by flash floods. By applying a magnetic field to the fluid a frozen flow is generated; and when it returns to the liquid state, the net continues to flow with the surface topology of the water.

Forged into the rock face is a vertical measuring instrument with a sliding float which records the fluctuating movements of the water as it flash floods seasonally. This information is sent digitally to the condensation node in the camargue. When the gorges flash flood, it causes a critical threshold to be reached, whereby the vacillating object begins to writhe frantically, like a wild dog on a leash. As the water cascades all around, the gut descends beneath the water and causes the sp(l)ine to coil up until it exerts its potential energy in a dramatic whip-lash effect.

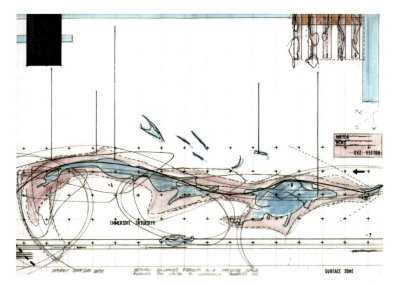

Section through Gorges Du Fier

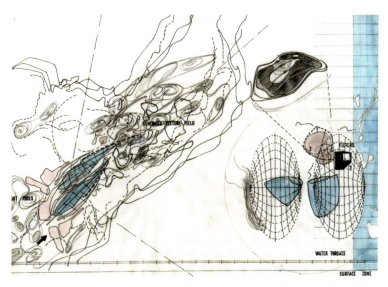

Aerial view of gorge showing Generated Texture Field

Earth
Cruas

Old stone houses huddled around an abbey, all covered with a fine white dust from the large cement works by the river. Not far away the great towers of the nuclear power station pour forth huge plumes of smoke. The land around Cruas is the thinnest part of the Earth's crust in France, and is subject to frequent movements, which might or might not become more serious.

This node is developed as an ecological retreat. The implicit challenge was to develop a process where the form would be suspended between the drawing and the environment but would lodge vividly in the imagination – a sort of psychological involution. A flat stretch of land was chosen, which is visually linked to the nuclear power station. The node has the simple program of exhibition and conference spaces which are occupied in the adjusted existing topology. This series of topological distortions blister the landscape into a field of giant looking sand worms which programmatically writhe.

The design was based on the metastable aggregation of architecture and information. The form itself is shaped by the fluid deformation of ellipses spaced over lengths of more than 45 metres. In the exhibition space, which has no horizontal floors, and no external relation to the horizon, walking becomes related to falling. The deformation of the land is extended in the constant metamorphosis of the active layer of the building which reacts interactively with the frequent earth movements. Visitors of the centre will be encapsulated by means of different light, touch and pulling sensors which cause this constant reshaping of the retreat.

The conference space is on three sliding platforms which migrate slowly around each other as a fluid deformation of space set on the reactive layer. The active layer becomes directly linked to the natural phylum and reactive layer explores the relationship between the natural and machinic phylum. These two layers restructure the external and internal skin of the building. The site becomes a play of dermic forces, the projected flesh or skin of the building spreads out, slips and bends like a surface of variable curvature on an abstract plane. If the seismic activity increases, there is the possibility that a critical threshold could be reached, whereby the elliptical structure will writhe frantically and cause subsequent contortions to the spaces. Enfolding the surface of the building which slowly but continuously destroys and reassembles itself though the direct relationships with this territory.

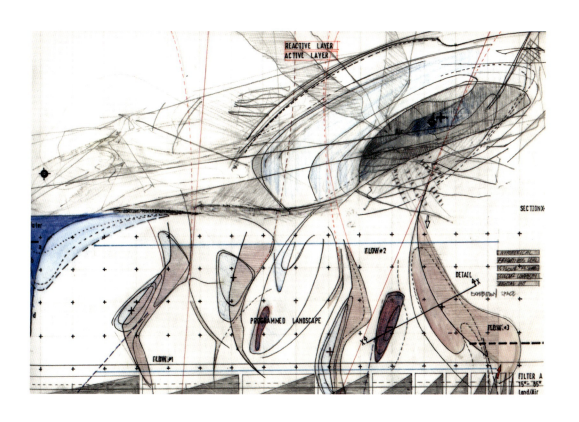

Preliminary sketch of Earth Distortions

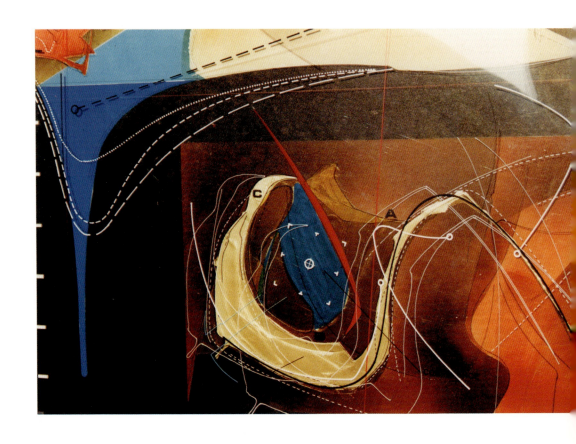

Aerial view of Ecological Retreat

Sectional perspective through Ecological Retreat

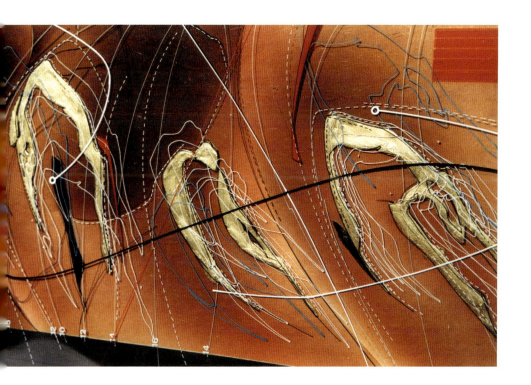

Fire
Chauvet Cave

On 24th December 1994, three speleologists discovered a cavern they believed hadn't been entered by humans in around 20,000 years. The Chauvet cave, as it is called, contains Palaeolithic paintings of lions, bears, rhinos and many other animals. Carbon dating has shown that some of the paintings in the Chauvet cave are over 30,000 years old. That makes them 3,000 years older than the oldest cave paintings previously known.

The physical intervention is sited in the Chauvet cave in the Ardeche region, where there is a vast network of galleries and rooms (about 500m galleries).

The receptors are a series of light sails cast out from the entrance of the cave. They trap and manipulate light on this open aspect south facing environment. The primary environment is the interface between the stable ecology of the cave and the more unstable exterior conditions. This is the place of restitution requiring the most advanced imagery and entertainment technologies. In addition museographic and educational equipment will recall the living conditions of prehistoric man, the evolution of natural environments and the origins of Rupestrian art. On this south facing entrance, a series of light sails are cast out and held about 10 metres up in the air on pneumatic poles. The surfaces of these light sails are composed of three layers. The primary layer consists of a muscle wire net structure that balances the movement of the photosensory cells. The secondary layer consists of a multitude of photosensory cells which focus the light on their photoreceptors; coupled with photodetectors which function as light meters in measuring light intensity and in clocking the hours of light and darkness. The timing of these photoperiods (light-dark) is related to circadian rhythms. The tertiary layer consists of a photovoltaic array which can rotate to the brightest part of the sky and is fitted with a microprocessor. All the receptors are focused onto a ring of amplified light.

The inflammable interfaces are developed to allow a personalised light to follow the user along the labyrinth of galleries and rooms. The second environment is the inflammable interface, which runs along the labyrinth of galleries and rooms. Here the user receive a backpack containing three telescopic armatures which can rotate in 3-axis of movement, one of which is for telescopic eyes and the other two are personalised light sources. Beneath is a footbridge with a smart floor networked to a light sp(l)ine overhead. The personalised lights are programmed to move around the cave walls sequentially framing specific cave paintings to enable the viewer to receive a personal dialogue with the drawing and environment. With the superimposition of four or five systems of projection, the cave becomes a dance of cacophonic geometries. Each time the user visits, they can chose from a multitude of programmed patterns of light on the cave paintings which will enable the user to look more intensely at the work and not to receive a repeated spatial and visual experience.

Under the stark glare of your personalised light a breathtaking backdrop unfolds: gigantic columns of white and orange calc-spar, alternating translucent and nacreous, splendid draperies of minerals, sparkling carpets... Scattered on the ground are the bones of bears; the walls are scratched with claw marks... Suddenly, the image of a white horse appears before you.

The telescopic eyes enable you to look at the paintings in detail without leaving the footbridge. Either side of the footbridge are posts which transmit a continuous beam of infrared light. If the beam is broken the two light sources will turn off. You will be guided by the light sources through the labyrinth of caves. A continuous signal from the light sp(l)ine monitors your movements through the cave; this enables the system to detect where you are.

The light cage encapsulates the user in a kinetic volume of caged light. The critical environment where the user becomes an active participant in this node is the light cage which encapsulates the user in a kinetic volume of light. The light cage is supplied with light from the light sp(l)ine. The proposed device is based in one of the back rooms where there are large polychrome panoramic compositions of paintings and engravings from 4–12 metres long. In the centre of this space there is an elliptical hydraulically muffled glass platform. There are two rotating surface mirrors that fan out a laser ray as the referential surface. The platform is connected to a computer system which displays a wire frame model of the room to the place of restitution. In this light cage a swarm of dots moves, pursuing one another, thus behaving like a virtual creature commanded by the movements of the platform. An increase in movement generates more light and the whole room begins to glow. There is also touch sensors set in the floor, and standing on them triggers a real-time projection from the other nodes. During electrical storms, lightning is conducted through light spikes located above the cave, which pulses through the light sp[l]ine into the light cage.

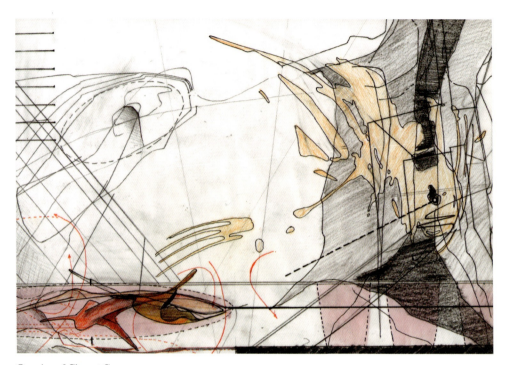

Overview of Chauvet Caves

Chauvet Cave Paintings

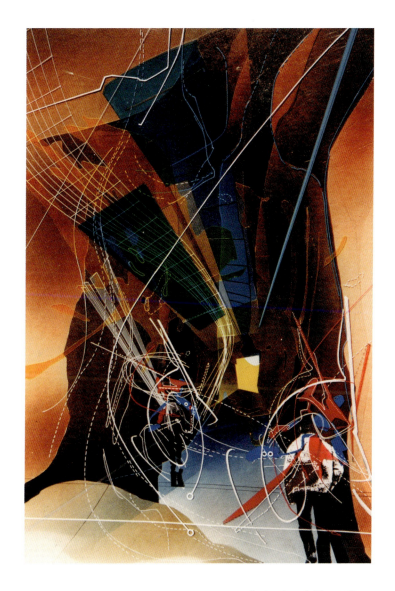

Section through Chauvet Caves

Air
Les Baux de Provence

On top of an isolated spur of rock, thrust out from Les Alpilles, and with steep ravines on either side, Les Baux de Provence is dramatic, beautiful, a shade sinister and melancholy. It is still tangled ruins, crowned by the wreck of a castle that seems to grow from the rock itself. The Mistral wind howls through the broken ramparts like banshees calling for vengeance.

The notorious wind of the Rhone Valley, the Mistral, blows for the most part between October and April. In winter the Mistral – its name comes from the Latin magister, and means master wind – can blow with tremendous violence. Icily cold, it screams down the Rhone valley from the north-west, with gusts reaching 130mph, tearing out trees, stripping roofs, blowing away cars. But the Mistral has its merits: it blows away clouds and dust, and keeps the skies of Provence crystal clear. In the past it was credited with preventing the fevers and diseases of the swamps of the Rhone delta from spreading up the valley. The Mistral is triggered by a set of specific meteorological conditions, one of which is the presence of a depression centred in the Gulf of Genoa, off the coast of northern Italy. The cold air coming down off the Alpine peaks get funnelled into the Rhone valley 'corridor'. It is at Valence that the wind gains strength and becomes the Mistral. Along the coast the Mistral often collides with the Garbi, a south-western wind, which blows in from Africa. The region is an impressive meteorological laboratory, an incandescent battlefield of meteorological conditions.

The air turbulence sits on the edge of the spur of rock. The combination of high mountains and the surrounding flat delta leads to a dramatic contrast in air temperature and wind pressure. Atmospheric inversion and turbulent air flows are common, resulting in high winds. The energy that these airflows yield is captured by strategically sited ribbon structures. Initially the ribbon structures are compacted in thin slots forged into the rock. The devices are programmatically triggered at different wind speeds, whereby a release mechanism catapults the ribbon structure out over the rock face. The ribbons are made in an aerofoil shape so as to produce enough lift to support the weight of them. The shape of the aerofoil is determined from the different trajectories of the wind. The ribbons are made up of a series of wind volumes which can expand at various rates of movement, depending on the different wind speed and pressure which is prevalent. Once the device has been catapulted out over the rock face, it calculates the wind speed and detects air pollutants and moisture content through a series of filters within the ribbon structure itself.

Broken Rampart

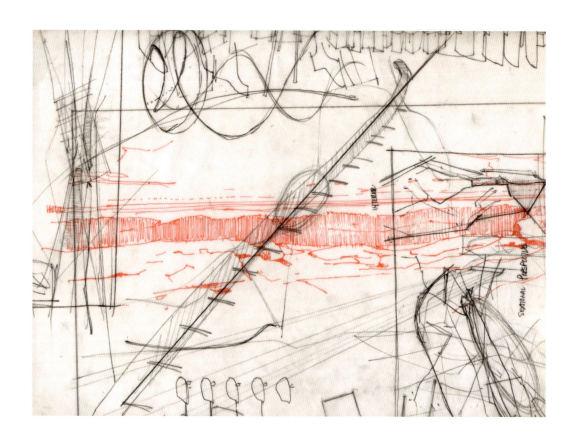

Preliminary Trajectories

Overview of Dynamic Ribbons

View showing Air Turbulence

Condensation
Camargue

This node collates and condenses the data from the other nodes to become the hub of the ecological research programme. The sensations, movements and emotions generated around the Rhone valley, and the data collected in the various nodes: These are ultimately channelled through this primary vessel.

There are a series of interactions, visual and kinetic between each of the nodes, blurring the threshold between the natural and artificial. This brief list views the potential of a distributed network within Water (N1), Earth (N2), Fire (N3), Air (N4) nodes.

The handrail on the gallery on N1 vibrates as a response to any seismic activity occurring on N2.

The generated texture field on N1 is animated within parts of the floor structure in the exhibition space on N2.

The wind pressure generated on the ribbons on N4 is regenerated with a series of miniature wind turbines fitted into the structure of N2, creating wind tunnels in the exhibition space.

Some of the sensors within the cave on N3 pick up acoustics, which are played real-time in the gallery on N1.

Some sensors on N4 pick up the howling of the wind, which is played real-time in the cave on N3.

Some of the sensors on N2 pick up conversations, which are played real-time on N1 and N3

The amount of light absorbed in the light sails on N3 effects the intensity of the silicon glow in cradle on N1.

Sensors on N4 pick up the changing intensity of wind flows, this information is digitally sent to N1 and the wind flows are translated into a visual image through a computer manipulation programme and presented down the phonoscope on N1.

Video recordings of the panoramic views on N4 and N2 are sent to N1, to be played real-time through the digital interface within the vacillating object.

Sensors spread out on N4 detect wind pressure, which is sent digitally to N1, where the information is translated into a series of movements within a smart gel in the back rest of the vacillating object. The interaction will occur intermittently with the existing pressure of the water.

Video recordings of the panoramic views on N4 and N2 are sent to N3, to be played real-time on to parts of the cave walls.

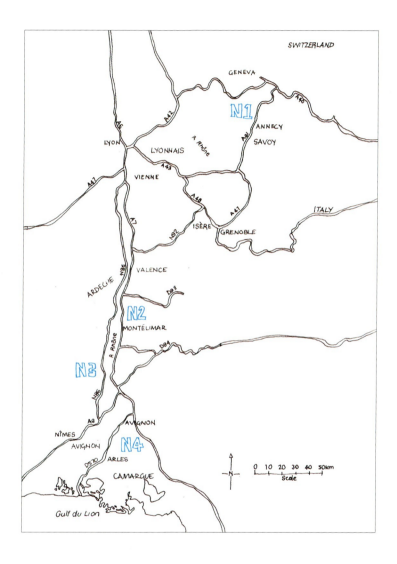

Map showing Rhone Valley

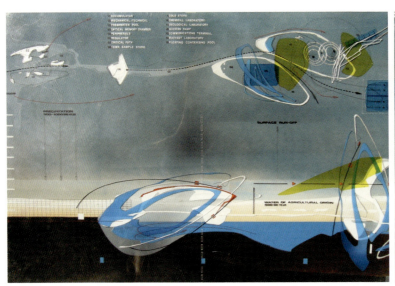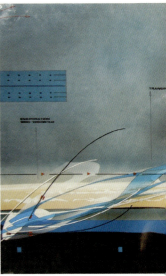

Sectional perspective through Ecology Research in the Camargue Lagoons

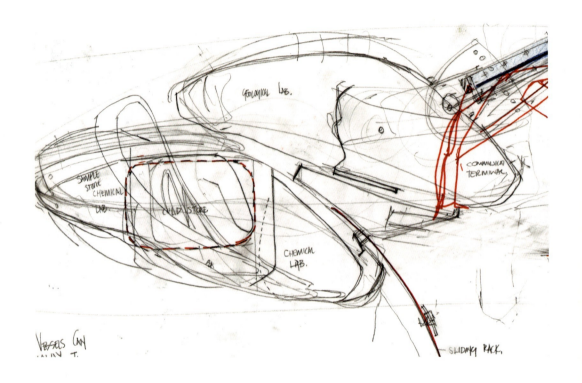

Detail plan through Ecology Research

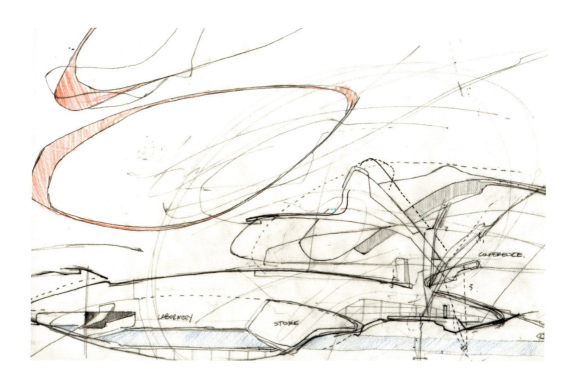

Section through Ecology Research

The Sansouire

The Sansouire

Nature evolves its own fluctuating systems, in which diverse ecological phenomena combine to create a fluid whole. What I have aimed to achieve is to develop an architecture as a machinic phylum, as expressed by Manuel De Landa. Thus, the natural becomes apart of the cultural potential of modern technologies. The architecture learns to respond and conduct a dialogue with the environment. This understanding enables the user to be plugged into the system at the nodes, the focal point, and the hub of the intervention. Elemental forces caress and tease the user with gently fluctuating movements. Yet, a shocking contrast is experienced when the system suddenly reaches critical threshold. The potential energy of these environmental forces manifests itself in violent and exhilarating disturbances in the tectonic and spatial fluctuations of the architecture.

The nodes discussed in this project are highly specified and intimately linked to each other in a complex web of feedback loops and retrosensing devices. The environmental and artificial disturbances create windows between each node. Ultimately, they are hybridised embryonic catalysts, whereby the user gains an intense alternative spatial experience within special locations and destination. It is not the real environment; not even with the object remembered but third imagined.

It gives voice to architecture because architecture is no longer an object of perception but rather a system of communications.

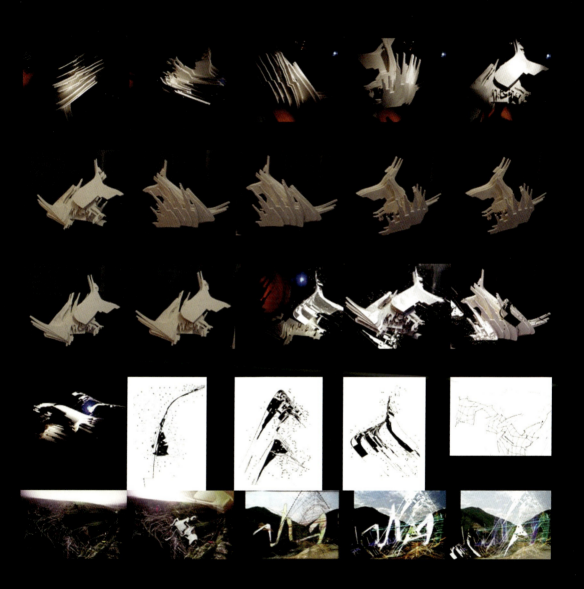

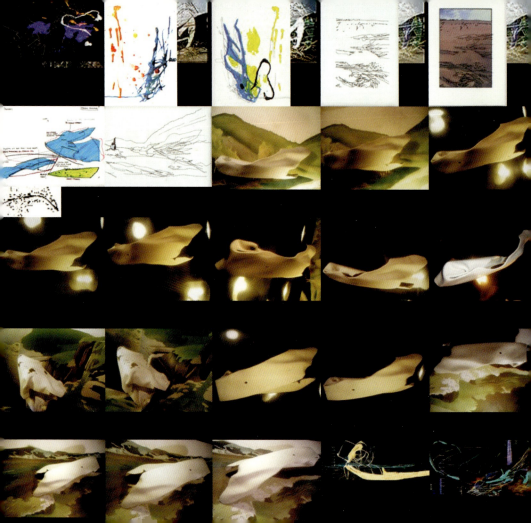

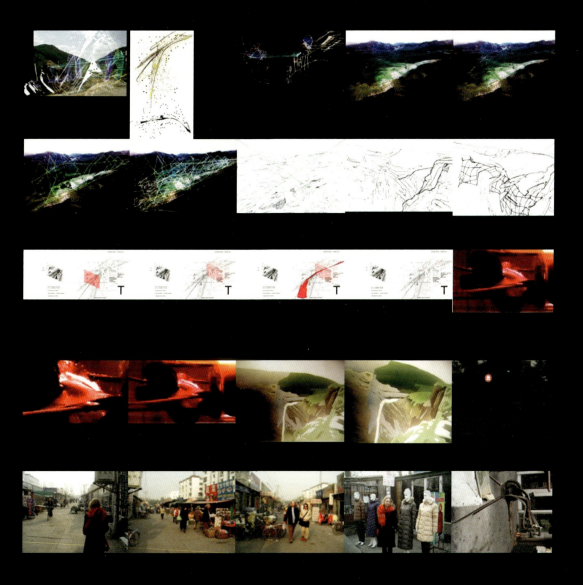

On Becoming Ecology

Between user – reader – space

If through the practice methodologies, as mentioned earlier, the drawing can handle communication involving multiple logical types. This methodology could allow for suspending the process along the continuum towards the development of form. The question could be: What is the impact of immaterial stuff on architectural form? What mechanisms can be provided to have an impact in the light of data? What processes can be developed to do it? Is it steps towards architecture on becoming ecology?

We can define ecology (a term originated by Ernst Haeckel in 1864) as the study of the relationship between drawing and the environment. This is to clearly specify what is meant by relationships and what is meant by environment.

There are many kinds of relationships between drawing an extremely important one is who communicates with whom and who instructs whom.

The concept of environment covers just about everything associated with drawing. No drawing exists without an environment.

The relationships of the biological and physical constituents of the environment together form a spatial unit, which is termed an ecotype. An ecotype could also define a unit that includes all of the drawing in a given area through research explicit and tacit so that a flow of energy leads to exchanges of materials between drawing and the environment within the system. In ecology the term ecosystem is used to both define a unit of study and to describe a concept or an approach. For instance, as a unit of study, the term ecosystem can be applied to a unit of landscape or segment of space and time. In a broader approach, the ecosystem concept provides a basis for examining environmental systems and their functioning.

In primary process, as discussed by Bateson, the focus of a discourse is upon relationships between things. This relationship is really only another way of saying that the discourse of primary process is metaphoric. Within the drawing and environment discourse, the metaphor retains unchanged the relationship which it 'illustrates', whilst substituting other things for the relata. The focus of relationship is, however, somewhat narrower than would be indicated merely by saying that primary process material is metaphoric and does not identify the specific relata. The subject matter of drawing and environment is in fact the relationship between user – reader – space.

Through the reading of Maturana and Varela one could define transfer from one medium, as drawing, to another, as environment, as in a material transfer or fortuitous transfer as structural coupling. Structural coupling establishes a clear difference between the ways living and nonliving systems interact with their environments. As Fritjof Capra describes, for example, 'when you kick a stone, it will react to the kick according to a linear chain of cause and effect. Its behaviour can be calculated by applying the basic laws of Newtonian mechanics. When you kick a dog, the situation is quite different. The dog will respond with structural changes according to its own nature and (nonlinear) pattern of organisation. The resultant behaviour is generally unpredictable'. A structurally coupled system is a learning system as it keeps interacting with the environment. Through certain research laboratories I have been working with, there has been a progressive development into a structurally coupled system between drawing and environment. Could we relate structural coupling as an approach for an architecture on becoming ecology, through looking at the Camargue ecology with its relationship of different states of form becoming an architecture of the machinic phylum.

In the development of form, we should not think of this process just as a set of changes in the architecture in a particular location but as a constancy in the relationship between drawing and environment. It is the ecology which survives and slowly evolves. In this evolution, the relata – the drawing and environment – undergo changes which are, indeed, adaptive from moment to moment. Bateson proposes that if the process of adaptation were the whole story, there could be no systemic pathology. Trouble arises because the "logic" from that of the survival and evolution of the ecological system. Architect Warren Brody, as early as 1967, characterized such behavior as a soft cybernetics that not only responds to its occupants but learns from them anticipating their needs. In Brodey's phrase, the "time grain" of the adaptation is different from that of the ecology. The relative constancy – the survival – of the relationship between drawing and environment is maintained by changes in both relata. But any adaptive change in either of the relata, if uncorrected by some change in the other, will always jeopardise the relationship between them.

In dealing with the theories on primary process, structural coupling and time grain and their respective link to the user – reader – space analogy one can refer to a quote from the renowned geneticist and biophysicist Mae-Wan Ho, 'To give you an idea of the coordination of the activities involved, imagine an immensely huge superorchestra playing with instruments spanning an incredible spectrum of sizes from a piccolo of 10^9 metres up to a bassoon or a bass viol of 1 metre or more, and a musical range of 72 octaves. The amazing thing about this superorchestra is that it never ceases to play out our individual songlines, with a certain recurring rhythm and beat, but in endless variations that never repeat exactly. Always, there is something new, something made up as it goes along. It can change key, change tempo, change tune perfectly, as it feels like it, or as the situation demands, spontaneously and without hesitation. Furthermore, each and every player, however small, can enjoy maximum freedom of expression, improvising from moment to moment, while maintaining in step and in tune with the whole.' (Mae-Wan Ho 1997). This quote is a theory of the quantum coherence that underlies the radical wholeness of communication between user – reader – space. This wholeness suggests total participation by the user and maximises both local freedom and global cohesion through the reader and space. It involves the mutual implication of global and local, of part and whole, from moment to moment in the process on disturbing territories.

Through the theories of primary process, structural coupling, time grain and quantum coherence one can challenge and develop the drawing to handle communication involving multiple logical types. The architecture on becoming ecology, on one level, may become mental landscapes of design which are modelled the way people think about their world through the designing mind and the drawing tool. The task seems overwhelming, but is not impossible. From our new understanding of complex biological and social systems we have learned that meaningful disturbances can trigger multiple feedback processes that may rapidly lead to the emergence of new order in design and practice.

My current research project A priori nature: constructing architectures consist of several still separate attempts to map a theory associated with drawing and the environment. As all of the attempts don't register in the state between, but are polemic in the territories to be mapped.

The focus will be discussed through the Basque project, which is about the praxis towards architecture becoming a coupled action with the environment by creating a genetic fingerprint through the drawing. What becomes is an object that is carefully crafted through technological, manual and environmental constraints. Through the determining effects of interaction between the environment and drawing, architecture will become the 'editor' and operate as space-scribers at the intellectual level of intuition and 'active' purposefulness. These constructs will be architectures of meaningless objects in featureless space.

"We are attached and engaged, indivisible from our world, and our only fundamental truth is our relationship with it." (Lynne Mc Taggart 2003).

In recent years there has been quite a bit of scientific research into communication and language through the drawing and environment connection between user – reader – space, which can help us to understand what it is and how it works. Is it usual, when believing oneself original, to reinvent the wheel. In architecture and thinking about these issues, this danger becomes particularly acute, especially in an ecologically sensitive age. Lynne McTaggart has written a useful analysis, The Field, which reveals a number of research findings to suggest that there is a logical truism: that is our relationship with it. This relationship is a trap lying in wait for unsuspecting architects who, like God, intervene in the world of natural laws and unfolding evolution trying to make environment or the world into a better place. Yet it is also very suggestive way of thinking about architecture that can be added to and, perhaps, altered. This approach leads us to the question, what is the relationship of drawing and environment in the field?

Coherence, as suggested by Mae-Wan Ho, could be seen as the relationship, which means that all elements are able to cooperate. 'Coherence establishes communication. It's like a sub atomic telephone network. The better the coherence, the finer the telephone network and the more refined wave patterns have a telephone. The end result is a bit like a large orchestra. All the elements are playing together but as individual instruments that are able to carry on playing individual parts. Nevertheless, when you are listening, it's difficult to pick out the instrument.' (Mc Taggart 2003).

Coherence in Architecture and their parts are still treated, for all intents and purposes, as machinery through diagrams and datascapes. In relation to design and architecture the user doesn't need to understand everything and break things down; it is all connected on an 'invisible web' where everything would be connected to everything else through a reader. This moves the debate away from a mechanistic view of architecture and towards an architecture in a holistic view.

Thoughts and constructs on coherence in architecture vary widely. Constructs in coherence could commonly be thought of as these terms 'sustainable', 'environmental' and 'conservation' all belong to the language of appropriation, suggesting that a degree of coherence is to maintain or prolong rather than be attached, engaged and indivisible. Coherent architectures are connected to a vast dynamic cobweb of energy exchange with a basic sub-structure containing all possible versions of all possible forms of matter. Nature is not blind and mechanistic but open-ended, intelligent and purposeful, making use of a cohesive learning feedback process of information being fed back and forth between elements of constructs and their environment.

Value

The value of this research is looking towards the coherent qualities for an architecture to be engaging and become wholly informed in all fields of knowledge and institutions that work with all sources of fieldwork data, environmental, social and technological through the process of construction. This approach is the part of the design process when the architect manifests their desire and aspirations- implicitly embracing user – reader – space as indivisible testing out morals and ethics through choice and chance.

The value to determining effects is to firstly, identify the research investigations in an environment and the particular analysis of that element under consideration. For example, how is the flora/fauna colony going to grow, change and adapt? This example is currently exemplified into a spatial model at research institutes, like Cranfield Ecotechnology Research Centre, which could form a strategic palette for an architect to develop an architectural process operating with an existing framework.

To enable and demonstrate this methodology for analysing determining effects of interaction within a field strategy, that is based on a complex systems approach should contain the following elements:

Engage with key processes of existing studies in the territory to be disturbed and link these indicators of field strategies within the design project through its respective eniatype which comprises of ecotype, notational, instructional and aesthetical strands.

Apply a response methodology for integrating the constructing effects of the proposal as drivers of change in the states between user – reader – space through the eniatype.

Enable the development of a proposal by implementing a dynamic spatial model of the physical processes through the eniatype.

Design and integrate a dynamic model showing the changes occurring in a target area, whilst interfacing physical and non-physical subsystems through the eniatype.

Together, these four elements distinguish the research from other projects on field strategy. They are important because they relate to major methodological research issues and questions that are faced by integrated research projects seeking generic approaches.

To practice new knowledge of how a type of architecture could become a fingerprint of its environment is my intent. A priori Nature: Constructing Architectures is an experiment in taking 'the field' to advance coherence in architecture during acts of construction.

Basque Project

The Basque Country (Euskal Herria in Basque) is a cultural region that straddles the western Pyrenees mountains that define the border between France and Spain, extending down to the coast of the Bay of Biscay. The project is the mixture of abstraction and singular history, necessity and chance, order and chaos that is so potent and engaging. It led me to present a prior nature: constructing architectures in three territories of the Basque country. Using the Basque landscape to 'narrate' this architecture is most developed at the origins – a source of rivers, raw materials and energy. The architecture becomes concerned with the unfolding of naturalness, to show this sequencing of nature as seen from the architecture. It is also one of transition, of an almost phantasmic, high altitude architecture that keeps on surfacing and disappearing in the landscape in its tireless dialogue with nature.

The actual Basque environment is studied through various eniatypes, with no predetermined awkward strategy. To imply proactive identifiable quantitative and qualitative constraints which are in the dynamic framework of the actual. In the Basque project three environments were chosen to consider. The first is the source of the river Nervion. This river flows through Bilboa, and at its source it dramatically drops 300 metres into the valley below. The second environment is in the Deba valley. In this province of Gipuzkoa there are six small rivers running almost parallel to one. These six rivers form valleys separated from one another by mountains, thus contributing to the fact that each region constitutes a microcosmos with its own peculiar characteristics. And finally the third environment is the Castillian plateaux in the territory of Alava. The key interest of these three areas was the research on the high concentration of heavy metals in the Basque landscape which still remains a serious threat to flora and fauna.

The drawings propose just one simulated eniatype of many, for that particular environment, for analysis of coherence of potential constructs. Currently the focus of the research is looking at different viewing angles, as represented by the drawings, to show different levels of coherence between the potential constructs. These eniatypes can be rotated and analysed through various shifting scales for more detailed analysis of coherence between constructs of the natural and artificial. To incorporate better coherence of constructs depends on the level of research available to be applied into this framework. This methodology will also test out the potential operation of the construct intended, so that the actual construct when sited does not have a predetermined usage.

Apriori model 01 Source of River Nervion

Scope

In defining scope, one was looking towards a report from the Environmental Department for the Basque country, which suggests that they don't really care about the environment and that business interests are so powerful as to be irresistible to the government, which prefers to industrialize their last wild places to reduce emissions while our consumption of energy grows. The other was researching dynamic observational data models from research centres, which have digital models of the three chosen environments. These anamorphic studies, as represented by the drawings, defined the scope of works to develop new eniatypes for investigation of these architectures in construction. Using an actual environment to narrate the potentials is particularly appropriate to refer to John Dixon-Hunt's 'zero nature'. Zero nature consists of non living rocks, water, equations, structural forces and diagrams. Each part of the process of these coherent constructs is to present its abstract laws and concrete moment, the duality of law and frozen accident. The drawings manifest such things as diagrams of nature – forces, laws, mental constructs, truths of the universe – that appeal to those who take the trouble to decode them. Phenomena will be abstracted from its environment and staged to allow the theory to be tested in a reproducible and communicable way. For example, at the source of the River Nervion, the curves derive from the analysis of data from the context and various functional objectives, but the underlying notation is derived from editing the way nature self-organizes into flowing fractals. The implications are to review the constraints of the environment and view the architecture in coupled action with its context. This view was intended to enforce the typical potential of the scope, as a connected whole, which would real-time enforce action on an architecture working at that prescribed level of investigation.

Coherent constructs

In relation to the Basque project, my intention here and elsewhere is to produce a kind of cross-coding between levels of constructs natural and technological. I have developed a work in progress diagram, which shifts dynamically and continuously redefines new states of eniatypes slicing backwards to show forms that are produced as a reflexive approach to the environment it is responding and editing architecturally. The resultant diagram becomes one of continual change and shifting analysis of different sets of coherence, progress and regression. The architecture becomes an active, projective affair of the technological environment within the precedence of the natural. It is espoused from the working model by redefining the coded notations to define solid/void, relative/absolute, rational/non-rational, reducible/irreducible, process/development. The landscape constructions mirror

Apriori model 03 Deba Valley

the early fusion of unbridled engineering ambition in the epoch of biophysics.

As Prigogine has stated, 'most phenomena of interest to us are open systems, exchanging energy or matter [and information] with their environment suggests that a reality, instead of being orderly stable and equilibrial, is seething and bubbling with change disorder and process. All systems contain subsystems, which are continually fluctuating. A single fluctuation or a combination of them may become so powerful, as a result of positive feedback shatters pre-existing organisation. At this moment there is a bifurcation point and the system will disintegrate into-Chaos or leap to a new, differentiate level-Order'. (Prigogine 1984).

Through the three proposed environments there is the capacity for regeneration through the various eniatypes. For example, in the source of the river Nervion accumulation of density in the eniatype nets would trigger a reflexive response to moisture content in the hanging algae which support a rare species of beetle. Following, would evolve in a series of architectural propositions to protect the moisture levels of the hanging algae. Within each of the environments there is demonstration of numerous species to regenerate as though a hidden blueprint were being followed. This approach allows for a reflexive quality of an architecture acting out its differences with its environment is to raise its profile and get closer to perfect coherence, which is a state somewhere between chaos and order.

Meaningless objects

Through these disturbances in the field what becomes is an actual construct – a construct with no definitive meaning – an architecture as primary process, structurally coupled, time grain within the wholeness of quantum coherence.

These architectures of the actual are determining effects of the actual with chance and necessity as the buoyancy aid. Depending on the intention of the architect, the constructs are connected in the field, so any adaptations and modifications will always be challenging through morals and ethics. As with Francisco Varela's view that the basis of mind is the body in coupled action. Can the view that the basis of architecture is nature in coupled action, that is, the field as a networked web establishes the constructs of a priori nature: constructing architecture as viable in situated contexts. From this perspective the architecture appears as a dynamical process and not a syntactic one of real time variables with a rich self-organizing capacity and not representational machinery? To understand the meaning of anything, we need to relate it to other things in its environment, in its past, or in its future. Nothing could be meaningful in itself.

Apriori model 01

Featureless space

Architecture can become the 'editors' of environments and operate as space-scribers at the intellectual level of intuition and 'active' purposefulness. The importance of this methodology is that we will be able to work with a variety of 'generating' tools at the conception of the project. This methodology would be a liberating and exploratory examination of testing morals, ethics and intuition of the individual and project teams.

A palette of space-determining constructs can be resourced during the act of creation and the architect can choose whether or not any of the determining effects are appropriate or detrimental to the design process. This methodology would mean 'construction' liberates the architect from any linear constraints of reading specific environments as they would have to edit out all the logical types if they decide to not engage with parameters which are not in their gamut of information. This methodology is to unleash architecture from there shackles of limits and linear determinist thinking. Through this discourse of constraints reflexive eniatypes all ensembles into the framework that generates an architecture of meaningless objects in featureless space.

Apriori model 08 Source of River Nervion

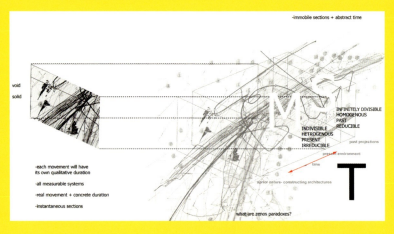

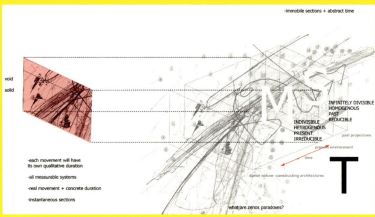

Apriori Model 05: construct process

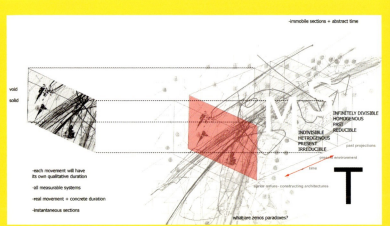

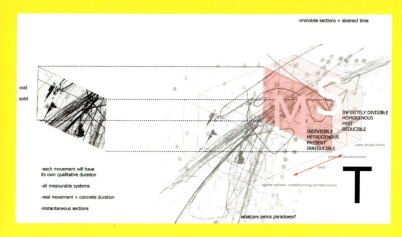
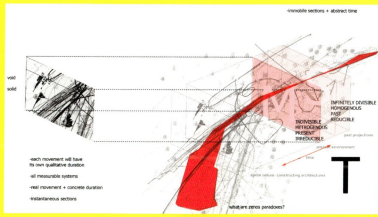
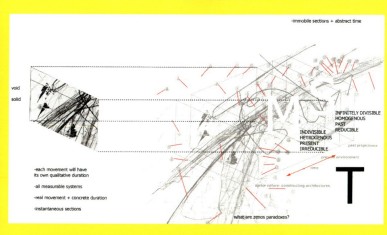

Archulus Ecology

Aldeburgh Coastline, Suffolk, England

Archulus posits a new landscape at the point where the local river meets the sea at Aldeburgh. The river is separated from the sea by a small spit of land which is prone to the rapid erosion; one day soon the spit will suddenly disappear and the coastline will flood. The proposition creates a series of almost cocked and loaded pieces that suddenly at the moment and point of breach explode into action. This landscape creates a new surface for plant and animal colonisation. The flood shields resonate in the territory of harpooning landscapes linked to each other through an enchanted tectonic loom embroidering and weaving spaces. Through the transitional territories of user – reader – space, Archulus explicitly injects and infuses its own agendas. The movement of waves, tidal imbalances and currents shape the ever changing Archulus profile. The relationship at the neck of the spit, between the water depth in the river and the sea will act as the source of power.

The coastline of Aldeburgh is a delicately balanced interface with the dynamic behaviour of natural and man-made processes. These processes operate over a range of time scales, from short term fluctuations to long term changes over thousands of years. Archulus was the consequence of recurring floods on the east coast of Suffolk, which loses more than a metre a year for the last 400 years.

A model is constructed between the environment and the drawing by using a set of derived values from the landscape [temperature, humidity, salinity levels, etc…] of the real world and from data and processes of the virtual world. Also from numerous techniques of capturing the real and casting it into the virtual. The model is fed time-based data through which the form becomes animate, the architecture vacillating.

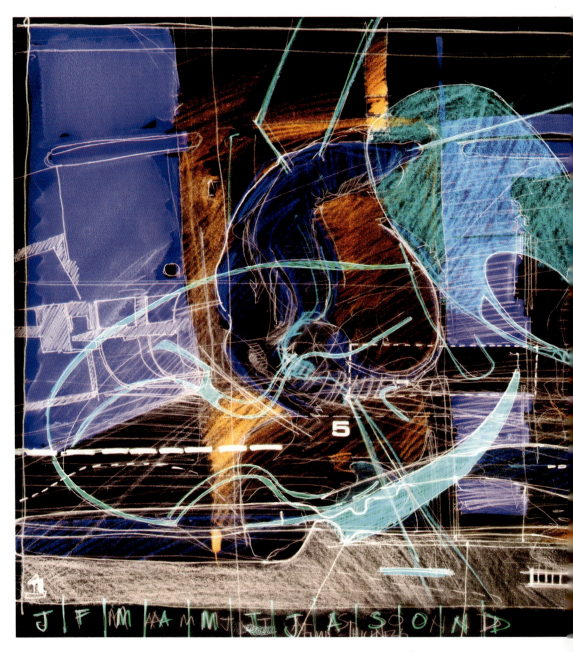

Sectional perspective through Flood Control Structure

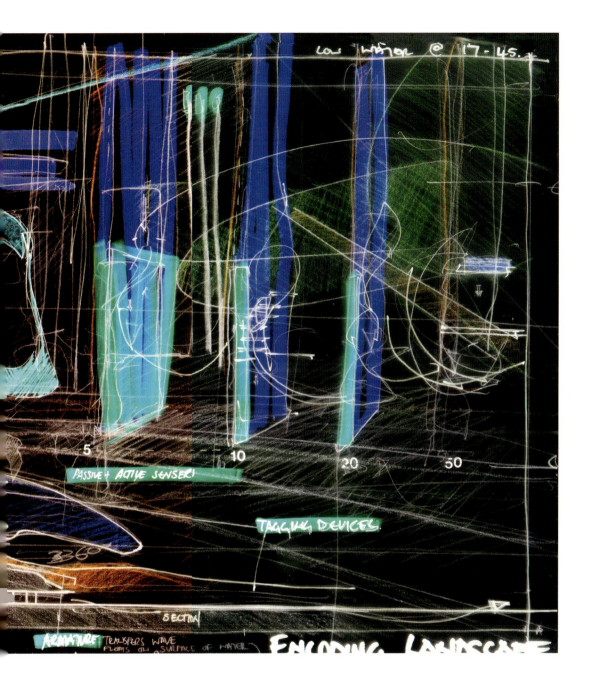

Harpooning Landscapes

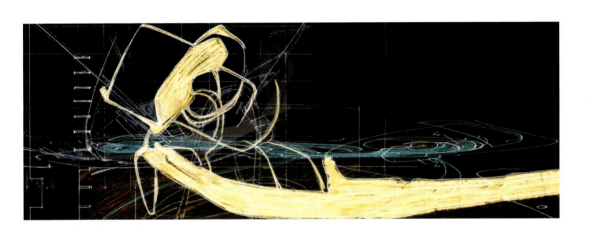

Flood Control Structure

Woven fibre-optic cables and circuitry flex with the movement of the structure. Filters reduce unwanted nutrients; dissolve gases, phytoplankton and waste, and pathogens which consume large amounts of oxygen. Mechanical aerators inject supplementary oxygen to prevent hypoxia harming the shrimp. Agricultural limestone and burnt lime adjust the acidity level of the water. A shotgun mechanism positioned at the base of the flood control structure fires out the turbulence voids during flood tidal conditions, whilst buoyant chambers aid the movement of the flood shields.

These shields run along the length of the coastline that rapidly reconfigure after flood tidal conditions. This reflex results in a catalytic task space which consists of a series of dynamic frames and shifting horizons in between the flood shields. These shields shift at varying time scales, depending on the archaeological, geomorphological and diurnal processes acting on the site. The positioning strategy of the initial flood control structures were sited through the median of a hundred years of mapping the coastline territory between high and low tide. The shield form is generated through suspending this process of mapping onto a series of splinear time lines stretched out along the coastline then lofted together. These flood control structures are sensitive guides in a dialogue with the ever changing coastline. They act as the arms of this enchanted loom, working with the natural phylum through the machinic to enable the flood control structure user to be apart of the environment through the readings of its pristine positioning in space. This lightweight structure filters nutrients as well as protecting and nurturing the advancement of secondary succession in the linked hyper polder.

At normal tidal conditions the shields are positioned in a low profile state – just a shimmering backdrop to events. But it is a surface of potential, carrying a latent charge, which may suddenly be released during flood periods. At the juncture of the flood shields is the nave which translates environmental stimuli from the surrounding landscape, and can dissolve into movement-supple fluidity or complex patterns. The translation surface responds to the landscape strategy, oscillating between solid and fluid. Within each nave is a suspended aisle which holds the archive of these communicating vessels from the turbulence voids, flood control structure and hyper polder.

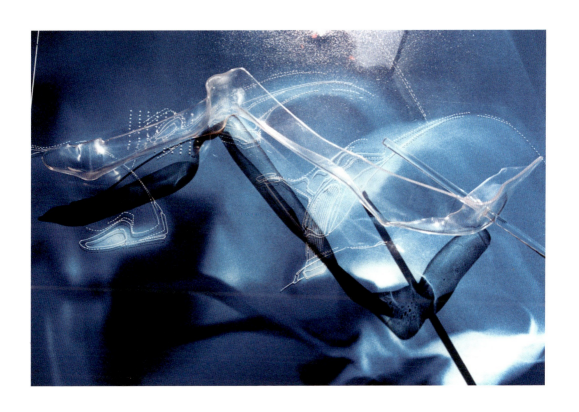

Model of Flood Control Structure

Sectional perspective through Flood Control Structure

Low slung perspective through Hyper Polder

Turbulence Void

The turbulence voids scan and map the territory of the seabed. Dark spaces and recovered, abstracted and observed. This territory will become the study of a renegade ecology, whereby the different levels of communication will be identified and distributed into an invisible framework. The processes of archaeology and architecture are used to strive for discovery of the old settlements and roman forts below the silted beds of the North Sea. At times this will be achieved through the drawing and will be exhibited digitally through the environment inside the suspended aisle of the nave; at other times a turbulence void will suddenly appear on the surface of the water and start skimming and agitating. During this time the turbulence voids will catapult out the generated texture field nets, which freeze in animated positions to temporarily reveal fragments of the discoveries in the murky sea.

Turbulence voids become the reader of this watery environment between user – space.

They are connected to the main flood control structure by a spool mechanism and have two main applications; one as a float structure and the other as a harpoon mechanism. As a float system the turbulence voids begin descending and drifting for ten days powered by the movement of the currents. Initially they scan the seabed floor for archaeological remains, lost churches and shipwrecks. The turbulence void registers these remains through acoustic positioning devices; every contour is scanned with a laser. As the turbulence void ascends, the information received can then be mathematically mapped and recreated in a virtual archive within the nave of the flood control structure. The device can move at varying speeds and trajectories, mapping these solids. It is trailed by a series of ribbons which act as light buoys on the surface of the water to warn off any nearing vessels. As a harpoon mechanism the turbulence voids inflatable chambers are deflated in the keel during flood periods to take on this dynamic role. They skim at high speeds across the surface of the water soon after being released from the shotgun mechanism within the flood control structure. Skimming at high speed across the surface of the water the turbulence voids then dive into the seabed acting as an anchor for the flood control structure. The tension builds up on the leads, and the whole structure is shunted forwards exposing a new hyper polder.

The turbulence voids detect trace chemical impurities in the shallow sea, depicting a structure of certain propositional, but proposition is not clear; some parts extend like telescopes, revolve, or fold in on themselves. A flowering turbulence void has an interactive quality. It appears as a third life-form going through endless transformations and has no fixed total image.

Turbulence Void harpoon mechanism

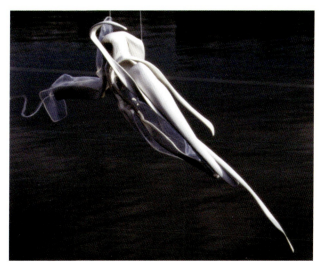

Turbulence Void float system

Hyper Polder

Colonisation on the Hyper Polder occurs during flood tidal conditions. It is encoded with a complex external skin, which acts as a filter for future harsh climates. The surface is thin and taut, deforming according to stimuli captured from the environment, which may be deployed as active or passive sensors. It is linked in to the base electrical services of the objects, such that all electrical activity can feed into its operational matrix, allowing it to register any aspect of electronic capture. Input from receptors of noise, temperature and movement will be sampled by a program control monitor which responds by selecting a number of base mathematical descriptions, each parametrically variable in terms of speed, amplitude and direction. This reflex produces a near infinite series of changing permutations, which overlap continually, drifting in and out of sequence. Topological deformations (cuts, mounds, ramps and ripples) render the surface a programmed landscape that not only has the capacity to fulfil the smooth functioning of the major programmes of aquaculture farming but also to foster the emergence of new and unanticipated configurations of space.

Hyper Polder formation takes place through secondary succession whereby a climax occurs when there is stability in transfer of material and energy in the hyper polder between plant cover, the physical environment and machinic phylum. This territory is initially uncovered for less than one hour in every twelve hour tidal cycle. The Hyper Polder is under constant transformation through two zones of development. Firstly, the slob zone, which is four hours, exposed everyday to the air in every twelve hours and receives new sediment every day. During the rest of the time this zone is waterlogged to the exclusion of oxygen and has a high Ph value. Secondly, the sward zone, which is four hours, submerged everyday to the air in every twelve hours and receives new sediment every day. Topological deformations in the Hyper Polder surface may remain where sea water is trapped then evaporates leaving salt pans. In the deformations the salinity level is too great for plants to grow. If 'disturbing territories' has emerged, it is the result of the journey towards it; were the journey to be made in reverse, the territory would revert back to the image of its incorporeal antecedent.

What matters most in the architecture are not the ideas as such but their resonances and suggestions, the drama of their possibilities and impossibilities. It becomes an architecture in search of physical form, but derived and controlled by the physical stimuli of this unique local environment. The work becomes the intermeshing of differential local stimuli in various natural environments, as control factors for the construction of architectural environments.

Photo survey around Aldeburgh, Suffolk, England

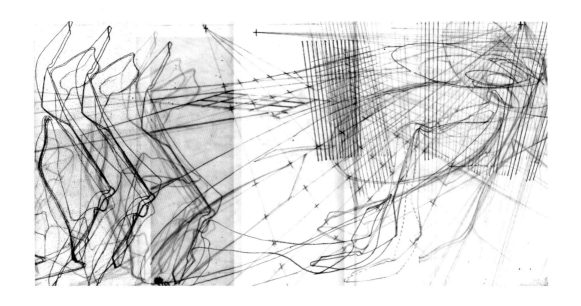

Low slung perspective through Hyper Polder

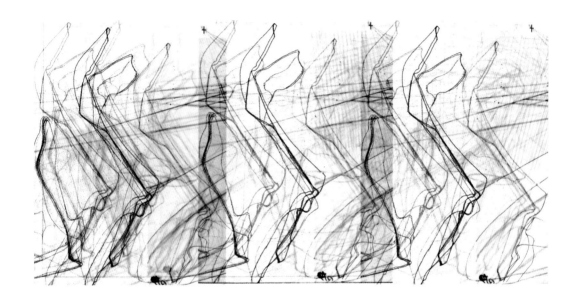

Sectional perspective through Flood Control Structure

Gardens of Hypotheses and Geomediated Meaning – Roy Ascott

Let us start from the point of view that all is metaphor, that there is no Ground of Reality on which perceptions are based; that, in short, we talk the world into being, that our descriptions are its becoming. The residue of that becoming, embedded in organic memory, data banks, and artefacts, finds its public signifier in the museum. The museum harbours its metaphors of reality from a raging semantic sea. Its fragments of past realities (shards of pottery, bones of dinosaurs) and its authorised metaphors of truth and beauty (scientific models, paintings, sculpture) all claim privilege as true representations of the past (or past representations of the truth), sanitised metaphors of world-views.

It is time to release the metaphors from their cages, to let loose upon the world these tight concentrations of hypotheses. We don't need museums; the world itself is constantly being 'museumised' as we engage in language, in scientific discourse, philosophical perspectives. The realities and worlds we construct by means of metaphor are thus fixed, taken out of the flux of dynamic transformations which constitute Life, and folded back in their concreteness as specimens, objectified, whose province then is the past. In seeking to explode the museum out of its cultural fortress into the world at large, we should attempt to plant Gardens of Hypotheses and Forests of Metaphors, as real, physical, sites for living, as an alternative to the tenements of reason, squares of certainty, and offices of determinism which congest our cities. Since the world is all metaphor, let us build metaphors of alternative realities in the midst of our material environment. As the museum dematerialises, we might then see new metaphors of what it is to be human, materialise all around us. Time for what can be called the geomediation of the museum: to put memory, metaphor and meaning into the landscape.

If, a century ago, Henri Bergson, philosopher of change and process, had been appointed Director of French Museums, our debate today would probably not take place, or at any rate would be of an entirely different nature. We would have had a century of musing on evidence of 'becoming' rather than collections of artefacts of what has passed. As it is, Mickey Mouse has taken world leadership in conserving the archaeology of urban culture. Europe, home of the museum, benefits directly from the care and consideration Mickey has shown us, in privileging France with a Disneyland. Just as the old museum, with its formula of display cases and cabinets, pedestals and diorama, endlessly reproduced itself, colonising the planet with its ideology of The Past, so Disneyland is everywhere now, in essence, in a state of franchise-readiness to replay myth and history.

It is not simply that the theme park is our 21st century museum but that the museum now aspires to the condition of a micro-theme park, complete with gift shop, restaurant, guided tours, fancy lighting, glitz and glamour. All of which simply masks the fact that the past cannot be re-presented. In simulating the past we simply create an alternative present. In this process, simulation is more satisfying than representation because it is less arid, juicier, more engaging. The theme of a park suggests activity, and theme parks can make room for interactivity, for wholesale participation in the creation of meanings. In place of museums we need to re-plough and reseed the ecology with new metaphors and hypotheses. Art is understood as a system of negotiation between the viewer and artwork in the making of meaning. But just as art in the past was thought to be concerned with authoring (the one-way channelling of meaning), so museums saw their business as that of authorising (a one-way system of validating and valorising). The idea was not that we might participate in creating our past but that the Past could teach us a thing or two. There can be a moral insistence about the museum, which is odious. Museums have been not so much concerned with viewing as with viewpoints. I foresee curatorial obsolescence: we don't need our histories or our cultures to be shaped by others, which is to say that we do not need history unless it furnishes us with a present. History is a medium not a message. In using the medium we create our own content.

Insofar as art has been concerned with meaning (and there is surely little else it has ever been concerned with, since beauty and ornamentation have never been semantically innocent, value-free or without significant form – every canvas, mural and architectural feature being soaked in semiosis), and insofar as the museums have housed art, they have been veritable 'maisons closes' of metaphor, keeping the best, most shapely, most intelligent and seductive metaphors and meanings, for our delight. Museums have always enabled us to go whoring after culture. Indeed, if I think of those edifices of culture and learning built in the 19th century (and still very much with us), with their use of decoration – chandeliers, rich carpets, patterned tiles, sumptuous staircases, carved panels, gilded frames, velvet wall-hangings, luxurious drapes, padded couches – each one has the distinct appearance of the greatest little whore-house in the world. It leads us to think of the ancillary behaviour which supports such enterprises: the pimping with art dealers and antiquarians. Jean Genet's 'The Balcony' could well have been set in a museum as a bordello.

What fails to fit with our contemporary sensibility, is not so much the privilege and authority that museums seek to invest in the metaphors and hypotheses which their collections of objects and specimens are thought to carry, but that they present material artefacts (concrete instances) at all. Ours is increasingly an immaterial world, a scenario in constant flux, with little or no consensus reality. The planet is a densely layered, multi-faceted network of interacting personal, social, economic, cultural, political and spiritual differences. We hold few hypotheses valid for any more than the microseconds in which their contexts transform themselves. Change is the root of our condition; all is subject to constant revision, realignment, reconstruction, reinterpretation and reformulation. Unlike the butterfly of the museum lepidopterist, we will not be pinned down. We resist analysis. Indeed, the living butterfly provides a useful metaphor of contemporary consciousness. We fly from metaphor to metaphor, from point-of-view to point-of-view, settling for but an instant. Not for us those all-too-solid beliefs, those in-depth visions of the Age of Reason with its robust certainty and Cartesian assurance.

For us, all is surface, surface upon surface. Not for us a single steady gaze, nor its tunnel vision. Ours is a holistic, bird's eye view of events and of ourselves, even of our body. While we can see its inner processes, we live increasingly outside the body, beyond the body, just as our mind is now mind-at-large. All this is exemplified not just by the widespread appeal of interpersonal psychologies, fascination with the paranormal, post-modernist theory or post-structuralist philosophy, but also by developments in high technologies, the infrastructure of telematic networks through which we re-see, re-think and re-create the world and ourselves. In this context, which is a global context, we are not only leaving our bodies, we are leaving behind embodiment as the primary measure and sign of reality. Through telematic networks our presence is distributed. We are both present and absent, here and elsewhere, all at the same time. It's not so much that embodied representation is giving way to disembodied virtualisation, but that we inhabit a syncretic state of being, which is, in Marilyn Ferguson's memorable phrase, "both both/and and either/or".

In this immersion in the immaterial that constitutes a culture of computer-mediated events, fuzzy logic, principles of uncertainty, undecidability and chaos, what place do repositories of old pots and pans, sticks and stones, bones and baubles have in our consciousness? What useful role can be played in storing, classifying and representing material 'evidence' of objectified hypotheses, in this immaterial culture? Cannot traces be stored in databanks, for realisation in mixed reality environments when demanded, allowing users to access cultural, historical memories as they will, creating their own associations, conjunctions, reconstructions and meanings? Foucault, from the centre of European culture, and Donald Horne, from its antipodes, have both exposed the autocratic sub-text of museum-mediation. First, in its proposing that there is a Past to which we should attend, or within which we should expect to find coherence. Then, that we should read its authorised meanings. Museums store material objects whose meanings they create in the supposed context of

Truth or Accuracy or Authenticity. They bear witness to the Past, to evidence of the past, as the repository of truth and meaning in past events; that the universe, in other words, makes sense. This supports the dream that there might be meaning and truth in the present, and that with the state apparatus of culture of which the museum is a part, we might identify what is true and meaningful 'out there' within the chaos and contingency of life. Such pious hope stemmed from that age which saw itself as Enlightened, which tried through its institutions and discourse to create a fixed, methodical and durable present, wise in ages-old truths, full of reason, certainty, based on absolute and eternal verities: the world as museum.

How at odds that is with our current sensibility: we celebrate the uncertain, the shifting, the transitory. We invest our world in the technologies and systems of the immaterial, the fluid and fleeting, the fragmentary, layered and discontinuous. Our hypotheses are transient and transformative. The cultural paradigm is shifting. No longer is art, for example, the product of a solitary, individual point of view – a unique, singular or discrete picture of the world – a framed and fixed finality of form or content. Too many codes and texts crowd in on its formation. In fact, the artwork may not exist necessarily as a material commodity. It can exist as a provisional assembly of elements in a media-flow, as transient 'difference' in dataspace, although always as 'difference that makes the difference'. The commanding metaphor of art shifts from that of a window into the world to that of a doorway into negotiable (data) space, a space in which we can create our own shared realities. In that space all sensory modes can be engaged. Images, texts, sounds and gestures co-exist in this hypermedia. To enter the media-flow is to change it. The user is the content; the interface creates the context, always to be renegotiated.

But within this transcendental, out-of-body, mind-at-large scenario of consciousness technology and virtual spaces, we should not forget Mickey Mouse. We may be anxious that Europe could be rendered into one huge theme park, a vast virtual space for the entertainment of American, Japanese, and, increasingly no doubt, Chinese visitors. A vast coast-to-coast museum of rotting antiquity and quaint charm: English villages, French cathedrals, Bavarian inns and Viennese waltzes, the whole of European culture as a vacation experience, a total entertainment. But perhaps Europe is a theme park, a virtual reality, in any case, its universities, hospitals and banks no more than worn-out metaphors for learning, health and order, with no reality principle there. Perhaps even these eternal verities themselves are simply linguistic constructs without 'essential' meaning or reality. If everything is subject to the rule of relativism, the shelf life of any metaphor is limited. Museums often prevent us from relinquishing metaphors once they have actually outlived their usefulness. Conserve, protect, curate a metaphor too long and it may become a truth, an evidential fact, a part of the jigsaw which can make up the whole picture. Such fictions are seductive. Against the museum, we must press the necessity to constantly re-describe and reconstruct reality, the many realities that are ceaselessly created within our universe of metaphor and meaning. For the artist whose job this is (and everyone can take this role on board – no genetic endowment is required) the world is all interface, awaiting meaning. In a sense, all worlds are virtual worlds, since everything is in a state of becoming.

Geomediation

Instead of museum buildings we could have knowledge landscapes – gardens of hypotheses to be planted, on various scales, within and around large urban centres. They will be seeded with ideas – physical, material analogues and metaphors of scientific and philosophical hypotheses. Thus, each garden landscape would offer a series of challenges and encounters. The journey through these landscapes might be directed (linear, chronological), wandering (associative, thematic), or haphazard (creative, speculative). Unorthodox, marginal, exotic, eccentric hypotheses would feature as much as strictly classical, accepted and academically respectable theories, principles and ideologies.

These physical metaphors could engage the visitor across the full range of senses (visual, acoustic, tactile), calling for participation and interaction at all levels. These analogues and metaphors will involve in their construction and realisation both traditional media and advanced technologies. Transdisciplinary teams of scientists, artists, poets, historians, and technologists would design them. The transition between scientific or cultural paradigms will be encountered metaphorically by such landscape ruptures as waterfalls, cliff faces, ditches, fences and portals with the passage between them assisted by bridges, ferries, swings and ladders.

There might also be erected a kind of data-termite mound, echoing the project for a "Pillar of information" that I proposed for Joan Littlewood's Fun Palace in the 1960s. As Stanley Mathews describes it in a recent study:
Certainly the most prescient proposal for the application of computer technologies was the "Pillar of Information," [that] would be a kind of electronic kiosk, which could display information of all sorts, based on the model of the Encyclopedia Britannica. His system was among the earliest proposals for public access to computers to store and retrieve information from a vast database. In addition, and even more innovative, it would also keep a memory of previous inquiries. As one person took information from the pillar, a trace would be recorded of the transaction, and subsequent users would be able to track the patterns of use, and the system would suggest multiple knowledge pathways, in much the same way that use patterns on the internet of today are mapped through the use of tracking "cookies".

Ascott envisioned that this would give users insight into the interests and queries of other Fun Palace users. Based on patterns of user interaction, the Pillar of Information would gradually develop an extensive network of cognitive associations and slippages as a kind of non-hierarchical information map, both allowing and provoking further inquiry beyond the user's initial query. The resultant web of information and free association to be produced by the Pillar of Information foreshadows in many ways the more recent rhizomatic theory of knowledge developed in the late 1980s by Gilles Deleuze and Félix Guattari.

In planning the Garden, the material means would be afforded by considerations of space and interaction involving natural media – grass, trees, lakes, hills, waterways, wind, sun; artificial media – prosthetic ecology, and cybernated structures and systems; virtual media – digital and post-biological systems and simulations; and telematic media – telepresent links with laboratories, research institutes, research sites, space stations, satellites, remote sensing stations... and other Gardens of Hypotheses.

Major sites might present in material metaphors clusters of scientific principles as they have appeared historically (Cartesian, Newtonian, medieval, classical, alchemical, magical, quantum mechanical, relativistic etc), always including in each cluster a number of different disciplines, alongside artistic or economic aspects of whole cultures. These clusters would represent scientific and philosophical traditions from many eras, across a diversity of cultures. Minor sites would consist of monuments, plazas, pagodas, tents at which little-known, marginal, esoteric or tentative propositions and premises might be encountered.

In addition to zones of reflection and contemplation, arbours for quiet reading, there would be encounters with 'knowledge activity' which would call for intense physical participation – climbing, swimming, crawling, swinging – with the material parts of a material hypothesis or metaphor, e.g. sliding through 'wormholes' between parallel universes, or 'enacting' the transformations in the lives of cells.

Visitors could gain a conception of scientific culture, of art and philosophy as being dynamic, paradoxical, shifting, disputational, growing, transformative, creative rather than staid, fixed, absolute, dogmatic. Visitors would experience the exhilaration of ideas, hypotheses and propositions which permeate world cultures, sense the creative potential of technological extensions of mind and body, and be stimulated and excited by sharing transformations of thought and perception produced in the scientific, artistic and philosophical domains. The Gardens of Hypotheses would be found all over the planet, subject to cycles of growth and change, reflecting always our changing perceptions of the world, and ourselves.

Bibliography

Bergson, H. Creative Evolution, Trans: A. Mitchell. New York: Henry Holt. (1911).

Ferguson, M. The Aquarian Conspiracy. Los Angeles: JP Archer. (1980).

Foucault, M. The Order of Things: An Archaeology of the Human Sciences. New York: Pantheon, and London: Tavistock. (1970).

Foucault, M. "Of Other Spaces," trans. Jay Miskowiec, Diacritics (Spring 1986): 22-27.

Genet, J. Le Balcon. Paris: Arbezat. (1956).

Deleuze, G. and Guattari, F. Capitalisme et Schizophrénie, tome 2 : Mille Plateaux. Paris: Minuit (1980).

Donald Horne, The Great Museum: The Re-Presentation of History. London and Sydney: Pluto Press. (1984).

Mathews, S. "The Fun Palace: Cedric Price's experiment in architecture and technology" Technoetic Arts, 3.2. pp 73-91 (2005).

© Roy Ascott 2005

Roy Ascott is Professor of Technoetic Art in the University of Plymouth. Founder of Planetary Collegium and director of CAiiA.

Glossary

Eniatype: that which comprises of ecotype, notational, instructional and aesthetical strands.

Information: any difference that makes a difference.

Interactionism: the term interactionism as used in the field of theoretical biology, has been refined through cybernetics, second order cybernetics, autopoiesis, complex systems, and alife (oyama). In general, the concept of interactionism in respect to observer and observed begins to define a system in semiotic terms. A semiotic system maintains that agents use coded information – material symbols – to pass on heritable traits. The subject of phenotypic transformations is of great interest and broad in scope. It is a subject that one might approach on the hand from a biological study or on the other hand from a phenomenological (Varela) or cultural/artistic study (Kristeva).

Logical Types: a series of examples is in order. The name is not the thing named but is of different logical type, higher than that of the thing named. The class is of different logical type, higher than that of its members. The injunctions issued by, or control emanating from, the bias of the house thermostat is of higher logical type than the control issued by the thermometer. The word tumbleweed is of the same logical type as bush or tree. It is not the name of the species or genus of plants whose members share a particular style of growth and dissemination. Acceleration is of higher logical type than velocity.

Machinic phylum: according to Manuel de Landa, for Deleuze the machinic phylum is the overall set of self-organizing processes in which a group of previously disconnected elements suddenly reaches a critical point in which they begin to "cooperate" to form a higher entity. The notion of a machinic phylum blurs the distinction between organic and non-organic life.

Meaningless: relating to something that has more than one meaning.

Neologism: is word, term, or phrase which has been recently created ("coined") – often to apply to new concepts, or to reshape older terms in newer language form. Neologisms are especially useful in identifying inventions, new phenomena, or old ideas which have taken on a new cultural context.

Palimpsest: a manuscript which has been re-used by scraping off the original text and writing over the top.

Phenomenology: a self-referential system. A method of literary criticism based on the belief that things have no existence outside of human consciousness or awareness. Proponents of this theory believe that art is a process that takes place in the mind of the observer as he or she contemplates an object rather than a quality of the object itself. Among phenomenological critics are Edmund Husserl, George Poulet, Marcel Raymond, and Roman Ingarden.

Phenotype: formed by the interaction of multiple genetic factors, not by any one of them in isolation; and all of them are expressed in a complex dance with the surrounding environment, air and earth and other organisms.

Progenitor: an originator or founder of a future development.

Relata: the relationship between things.

Syncretism: syncretism is the attempt to reconcile disparate, even opposing, beliefs and to meld practices of various schools of thought.

Tautology: a logical tautology is a statement that is true regardless of the truth of its parts. For instance, "Either it is raining now outside or it is not raining now outside" is a tautology. The opposite of a tautology is a contradiction, which is a statement that is always false regardless of the truth values of its parts.

Bibliography

Bateson, Gregory. 1972. Steps to an Ecology of Mind. New York: Ballantine Books.

Bateson, Gregory. 1979. Mind and Nature: A Necessary Unity. New York. Bantam Books

Borges, Jorge Luis. 1970. Labyrinths. London: Penguin Books.

Brodey, Warren. 1967. "The Design of Intelligent Environments: Soft Architecture." Landscape, Autumn, 8-12.

Butler, Samuel. 1915. Book of the Machines, Erewhon (1872). London: A.C. Fifiled.

Capra, Fritjof. 2003. The Hidden Connections: A Science For Sustainable Living. London: Flamingo.

Dixon-Hunt, John. 2002. Greater Perfection. London: University of Pennsylvania Press.

Ho, May Wan. 1997. "The New Age of the Organism." New Science = New Architecture, Architectural Design.

Kauffman, Stuart. 1995. At Home in the Universe: The Search for the Laws of Self-Organization and Complexity. New York. Oxford University Press.

Kelly, Kevin. 1994. Out of Control: The New Biology of Machines, Social Systems, and the Economic World. Addison-Wesley Publishing Co.

Maturana, Humberto and Varella, Francisco. 1987. The Tree of Knowledge: The Biological Roots of Human Understanding. Boston: New Science Library, Shambhala.

Mc Taggart, Lynne. 2003. The Field. London: HarperCollins Publishers.

Prigogine, Ilya and Stengers, Isabelle. 1984. Order Out of Chaos: Man's New Dialogue with Nature. Toronto: Bantam Books.

Spiller, Neil. (ed). 2002. Cyber_Reader: Critical Writings for the Digital Age. London & New York: Phaidon.

Further reading

Ascott, Roy. (ed). 2002. Art Technology Consciousness. Bristol: Intellect.
pp 139-144 Disturbing Territories.

Ascott, Roy. (ed). 2005. Engineering Nature. Bristol: Intellect.
pp. Breeding, Feeding, Leaching.

Spiller, Neil. (ed). 2002. "Reflexive Architecture." London: Architectural Design, Vol 72 No 3 February pp 56-63 Archulus: Flood Structure and Front Cover.

Spiller, Neil. (ed). 2001. "Young Blood". London: Architectural Design, Vol 71 No 1 February. pp 36-43 Shaun Murray.

University College London. 2000. Bartlett Book of Ideas. London.
pp 78-79 Camargue Condensations.

2000. "Offentliga RUM". Stockholm: No 2, March.
pp 42-45 Disturbing Territories.

Spiller, Neil. (ed). 1999. "Architects in Cyberspace II."
London: Architectural Design. pp 91 Phenoscape.

Conclusion

"The user is the content; the interface creates the context, always to be renegotiated."
Roy Ascott

Our times are such that we seek different forms of communication through our ecotype, notational, instructional and aesthetical interfaces. That is true of territories, which disturb the boundary lines of our individuality – our very sense of separateness with the built environment. As a designer we are constantly renegotiating in the natural and artificial environments. This kind of reality exists by no means in the future but is here with us now. It is not limited by time but exists now with its own operations as something which is somehow expedient. It is a direct intervention in the quality of the world, a space in which beauty acts. This point is inseparable from a deviation (clinamen), produced at the moment at which the territory is disturbed by, the point of contact. Through the point of contact a renegotiation takes place, as expressed earlier, one is the notion of a building existing in the form intended as a result of complex inter-relationship with it, or through it, or on it, where the building itself exists in the relationships between things, not the thing themselves.

When confronted between the renegotiation of user – reader – space with several alternatives usually one is chosen and the other eliminated. Through the book I have chosen simultaneously – all of them – to create, diverse futures for diverse times which they proliferate and fork. (Jorge Luis Borges 1970).

This forking that creates can come from fluctuating algorithms, selfish genes and algorithmic conversation theory which are concerned with the issues of territories. The line to be renegotiated is constantly disturbed. For example, in conversation, we continually renegotiate spaces of any difference that makes a difference.

Our framework here provides the designer with a view to on becoming progenitor in the ecology of design. It is clear that renegotiation of user – reader – space constitutes components. Each of which is connected to other disciplines concerned with communication, information and dialogue in our environments. Therefore, the framework provides us with a fundamental basis from which ecological design could be approached.

The work is about the methodologies through the designers of spaces and objects that operate inside them. We might use spaces at infinite scales (a scalar) and the mappings, both procreative and surveying that these methodologies can be constructed within the renegotiation of territories.

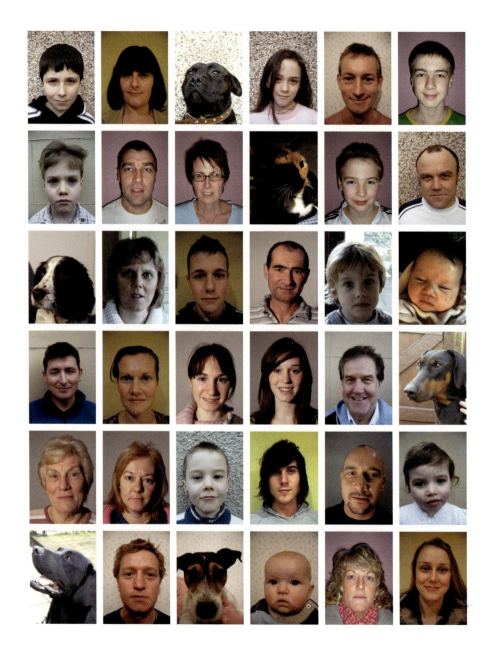

My Thanks

Will Alsop
Lynwen Anthony
Roy Ascott
John Coward
Patrick Ehrhardt
Wolfgang Fiel
Dene Grigar
Tesoc Hah
Charlotte Harrison
James Moore
Stuart Munro
Jerome O'leary
Esther Ortmann
Melanie Perkins
Kyell Peterson
Michael Phillips
Steven Pickthall
Michael Punt
Ala Pratt
Felix Robbins
Alison Sampson
Karin Søndergaard
Chris Speed
Neil Spiller
Tomas Stokke
Tim Thornton
Tony Thornton
Phil Watson
Claudia Westerman
Katharine Willis
Malin Zimm

Shaun Murray March 2006